T...
Person-Centred
Counselling
Primer

Pete Sanders

PCCS BOOKS
Ross-on-Wye

First published in 2006
Reprinted in 2008

PCCS BOOKS Ltd
2 Cropper Row
Alton Road
Ross-on-Wye
Herefordshire
HR9 5LA
UK
Tel +44 (0)1989 763 900
www.pccs-books.co.uk

The Person-Centred Counselling Primer

A CIP catalogue record for this book is available from the
British Library

ISBN 978 1 898059 80 6

Cover design by Old Dog Graphics
Printed by Athenæum Press, Gateshead, UK

CONTENTS

INTRODUCTION   1

Chapter 1   **THE ORIGINS OF PERSON-CENTRED COUNSELLING**   6

Chapter 2   **PERSONALITY**   16

Chapter 3   **THE ACTUALISING TENDENCY**   25

Chapter 4   **PSYCHOLOGICAL CONTACT**   33

Chapter 5   **THE CLIENT NEEDS HELP**   43

Chapter 6   **THE COUNSELLOR IS READY TO HELP**   51

Chapter 7   **UNCONDITIONAL POSITIVE REGARD**   58

Chapter 8   **EMPATHY**   65

Chapter 9   **THE CLIENT FEELS UNDERSTOOD AND ACCEPTED**   74

Chapter 10   **BEING NON-DIRECTIVE**   80

Chapter 11   **THE PROCESS OF CHANGE**   86

Chapter 12   **PERSON-CENTRED COUNSELLING TRANSCRIPT**   93

Chapter 13   **APPLICATIONS OF PERSON-CENTRED COUNSELLING**   98

Chapter 14   **RESEARCH INTO PERSON-CENTRED COUNSELLING**   102

Appendix   **RESOURCES FOR LEARNING**   109

GLOSSARY   111

REFERENCES   115

INDEX   122

ACKNOWLEDGEMENTS

Any book is the product of teamwork and I have been fortunate in having a number of folk help with this one. I thank the following people for feedback on progressive drafts as I slowly adjusted the book to its intended readership; Heather Allan, Moira Bishop, Suzanne Keys, Will Loynes, Jean Ransome, Maggie Taylor-Sanders and Wendy Traynor.

I am pleased to have Mick Cooper as joint author of Chapter 14 on research.

INTRODUCTION

Before we launch into person-centred ways of working, it might be helpful to take a look at some definitions of counselling itself. It is important to locate the helping activity of counselling in relation to other helping activities in order to avoid confusion regarding the purpose of this book. This book is specifically aimed at people wanting to learn about person-centred counselling with no previous experience or knowledge of counselling or psychology. The key word here is counselling.

So what do we mean by counselling?

What is counselling for?

One way of defining counselling is to look at what it is useful for. In the past thirty years, counselling has become ubiquitous, and it is perilously close to being presented as a panacea for just about everything. Some critics say that the emerging 'profession' of counselling has much to gain for claiming, on behalf of counsellors and therapists, that counselling is good for everything. It would be wrong to make such claims: counselling has its limits and part of being a counsellor is to know what those limits are. The problem is that when we are in distress, it is comforting to think that there is a simple answer around the corner.

The situation is not made any easier when we understand that simply sitting down and taking time out from a busy life can make things seem better. Counsellors must be able to explain to their clients the differences between this very important relief and comfort that can be gained from compassionate human contact on the one hand, and counselling as a specialist activity on the other. Counselling can help people in certain states of distress and usually involves change:

   • change in the way the client sees things or themselves

- change in the way a client thinks about things or themselves
- change in the way a client feels about things or themselves
- change in the way a client behaves

Although many people will not be able to put it neatly into a few words, what they seek from counselling can be roughly summarised in a few categories:

- support
- recovery
- problem-solving
- gaining insight or self-awareness
- developing new strategies for living

The sort of distress that counselling can help is often called 'emotional' or 'psychological' and can include:

- stress—a very general and possibly over-used term, but there are some situations in life, especially those that you can't control, that might leave you feeling so stressed that it interferes with your everyday life
- conflict—at home or work
- bereavement—whether a relative or friend. Indeed, having anything permanently taken away might lead to a feeling of bereavement, such as losing your job or losing your ability to do something like walk, play sport or have sex
- depression—another over-used term and not one to be taken lightly. Many life events can make us feel low, and talking it over really does help. The popular term 'depression' can cover everything from feeling understandably low after having your purse stolen or losing your job, through to being unable to get up in the morning or eat properly because you think life is not worth living
- coping with poor health, e.g. having a long-standing health problem or receiving a diagnosis of a serious or terminal illness
- trauma, e.g. surviving (including witnessing) something very disturbing (including abuse of various forms)

What counselling is not for

When someone decides to attend counselling sessions, they are, by definition, distressed. It is, therefore, particularly important that the client doesn't have either their time wasted or their distress increased by attending something that we might reasonably predict would be of no help.

As we have already seen, it is difficult to honestly predict whether counselling will definitely help in a particular circumstance. Nevertheless there are times when counselling is clearly not the first or only appropriate INTERVENTION. It is doubly difficult to appear to turn someone away when they arrive because sometimes:

- part of their distress might be that they have difficulty feeling understood and valued
- they may lack self-confidence and a rejection would damage it even more
- they have been to other types of helper and they think that counselling is their last hope
- they are so desperate they might consider suicide

However difficult it might be, we have to be completely honest with clients if we think counselling is not going to help. It would be wrong to let them find out after a number of sessions, after which they might feel that they are to blame for not trying hard enough. The use of counselling should be questioned if it is likely that their symptoms of distress are caused by:

- poor housing or homelessness
- poverty
- lack of opportunity due to discrimination or oppression

Problems of this nature are best addressed by social action. The counsellor as a citizen shares responsibility with all other members of society to remove these blocks to peoples' physical and psychological well-being.

It would be convenient if we could divide problems up into two neat categories; those of psychological origin (and amenable to counselling) and those of non-psychological origin (and therefore not amenable to counselling). However, there are some other causes of distress which, although they will not be *solved* by counselling, will undoubtedly be helped by counselling in that the person concerned will be able to function better with the kind of support that counselling can provide. It may also be that the client experiences repetitive patterns of self-defeating thoughts and behaviour which renders them less effective in dealing with problems which do not have a psychological origin. It might also be that a person would be better able to challenge an oppressive system if they felt personally empowered, and counselling can sometimes achieve this. Such problems include those caused by:

• poor health (a physical illness or ORGANIC CONDITION)
• oppression and discrimination, including bullying
• living in an abusive relationship

Counsellors must be constantly vigilant to ensure that their work with a particular client or clients in general is not contributing to disadvantage, abuse and oppression by rendering people more acceptant of poor conditions, whether at work or at home.

> Psychologists must join with persons who reject racism, sexism, colonialism and exploitation and must find ways to redistribute social power and to increase social justice. PRIMARY PREVENTION RESEARCH inevitably will make clear the relationship between social pathology and PSYCHOPATHOLOGY and then will work to change social and political structures in the interests of social justice. It is as simple and as difficult as that! (Albee, 1996: 1131, cited in Davies & Burdett, 2004: 279)

What is 'personal growth'?

Counselling in the UK has become associated with what might be called the 'personal growth industry'. Self-improvement has been a feature of our society for a hundred years or more and includes such initiatives as the Workers' Education Association supporting the educational needs of working men and women. More recently further education has embraced more non-vocational courses and reflects the fact that as we get more affluent we have to attend less to the business of mere survival. We can turn our attention to getting more out of life and along with other self-development activities, improving our psychological well-being proves to be a popular choice. Furthermore, when people have a good experience as a client, they sometimes see that learning to be a counsellor could be a further step in self-improvement.

This 'personal growth' use of counselling contrasts with counselling as a treatment for more acute forms of psychological distress as listed on pages 2 and 3 above. It is, however, no less worthy or ultimately useful. Fulfilled, happy citizens, relating positively to themselves and others, able to put good helping skills back into their communities are an asset, not a handicap.

USING THE GLOSSARY

You may have noticed that some words are set in SMALL CAPITALS. This indicates that the glossary on page 111 carries a brief definition and explanation of the term. The SMALL CAPITALS can appear anywhere in the texts, quotes, subtitles or index.

1

THE ORIGINS OF
PERSON-CENTRED COUNSELLING

EARLY YEARS

Person-centred counselling was originally developed by Carl
Rogers in the late 1940s and it continues to develop in terms of
theory and practice today. Rogers changed the name of his
approach over the years, starting with 'Non-Directive Therapy',
in 1942. In 1951 he preferred the term 'Client-Centred Therapy'
and in the 1960s when he applied the principles of his approach
to education, management, groups and conflict resolution, he used
the term 'Person-Centred Approach'. In the UK now it is most
common for people to describe themselves as a person-centred
counsellor or person-centred therapist.

Although Carl Rogers wrote (and co-wrote) around 20 books—
the most important (covering the theory and practice of person-
centred counselling) are referred to in this book in various places.
The following four works are pretty much essential reading if you
are going to attempt a diploma or degree-level course in counselling.

1951 *Client-Centered Therapy*. (Book, published by Constable
and Robinson, ISBN 1841198404.) This was Carl Rogers'
first major theoretical statement. It was written in 1950s'
psychological language and will be a difficult read for people
without previous experience or a social sciences background.

1957 *The necessary and sufficient conditions of therapeutic
personality change.* (Scientific paper, available in *The Carl
Rogers Reader* edited by H Kirschenbaum and VL Henderson
published in 1990 by Constable and Robinson, ISBN
0094698406.) This paper was actually written after the 1959
chapter but the latter was delayed in the publication process.
It is not quite as technical as the 1951 book. The paper outlines
the conditions required for therapeutic change in any
relationship-based approach to counselling.

1959 *A theory of therapy, personality and interpersonal relationships, as developed in the client-centered framework.* (Chapter in a book edited by Sigmund Koch in 1959 and now available only in a shortened form in *The Carl Rogers Reader*—see above.) This chapter is Rogers' most complete theory statement. He outlines in detail the theory and practice of client-centred therapy or person-centred counselling. All of the major concepts are defined in a language that, in technical terms, is somewhere between the 1951 and 1957 writings. Unfortunately a whole section of important definitions was omitted from the *Carl Rogers Reader* version.

1961 *On Becoming a Person.* (Book, published by Constable and Robinson, ISBN 1845290577.) This is probably the most widely-known and accessible of Carl Rogers' writings. It does not cover the technicalities of theory and practice, but many people find it a relatively easy and inspirational book to read.

If you do not have a psychology degree or a social science background some of these writings might be a little hard going. If you want to read more about person-centred counselling after finishing this book, there is a list of further reading on page 110.

Rogers' six conditions for therapeutic change

In his main theoretical writing in 1959, Rogers outlined the now famous six conditions for therapeutic change. Here he described the conditions which needed to be present before a client in therapy could change for the better. Rogers wrote another much shorter paper in 1957, again describing these 'necessary and sufficient' conditions. (There are some subtle differences between the two versions but they are not substantial enough for us to have to look at them here.) The conditions are:

1. That the counsellor and client make psychological contact.
2. That the client is vulnerable or anxious, i.e. sees themselves as being in need of help.
3. That the counsellor is more integrated and balanced than the client and can therefore be genuine, or as Rogers puts it, can

accurately 'be himself in the relationship'.

4. That the counsellor experiences acceptance, non-judgemental warmth or in Rogers' terms *unconditional positive regard* (UPR) towards the client.
5. That the counsellor is empathic towards the client.
6. That the client experiences these qualities of empathy and UPR from the counsellor.

In your studies you may come across the three so-called 'core' conditions of empathy, congruence and unconditional positive regard. These three conditions have been presented on their own over the years in order to simplify the theory and practice of person-centred counselling, but many people now think that it has not been helpful to do this. Separating the therapeutic conditions into 'core' and 'other' allows a number of misunderstandings about person-centred therapy, so I have included all six in this book.

Some writings refer to the 'core' conditions as the 'therapist-provided conditions' and although this might appear to make some sense, it is unnecessary and problematic. The problem is that it gives the impression that therapy is something the counsellor *does* to the client, i.e. the counsellor performs a set of behaviours and the client sits and receives them. In terms of person-centred theory, however, the six conditions *must* be taken together because therapeutic change can only take place in a *relationship*, i.e. both client *and* counsellor bring something. So the client and counsellor *together* make the change happen: they both bring essential ingredients to make the active therapeutic moment possible.

This is important because it helps us think about helping as a *relationship* right from the start. This is different from some other therapeutic approaches in which the client is seen as someone in receipt of *treatment* by an *expert*: the counsellor. It can also lead to the client not being seen as a person, but rather as a thing, a machine or computer to be fixed by using knowledge in a step-by-step procedure from a manual. These ways of thinking about counselling do not fit in with the fundamental principles of person-centred counselling.

Since the person-centred approach to counselling is based on the helping properties of the relationship to which the counsellor must bring essential qualities, it is only useful to think about the relationship conditions as *separate* factors in an abstract sense or *in theory*. When it comes to the practical activity of person-centred counselling, it makes more sense to see the counsellor as bringing these qualities as one complete attitude to a helping relationship, not a collection of separate conditions.

It is important to understand that these relationship conditions are *attitudes* not skills. In today's world where skills and competencies are at the heart of measurement in all kinds of helping settings, you might wonder how a therapeutic method can be based on attitudes not skills. When it comes to building relationships and working in a setting where people rely on you to be trustworthy, honest and accepting, it is simply a fact of life that we all experience these qualities as being deeper than superficial skills. The idea that your counsellor is nothing more than a skilled technician, employing skills to manipulate your feelings (albeit to your benefit) is just not palatable for many clients. It would appear that we want things in that caring relationship to ring true. We require our counsellor's caring to be professional and effective on the one hand, but also *authentic*.

Such fundamental requirements come only from deeply held attitudes, not from superficially learned skills. Clients can spot an inauthentic helper quickly and at some distance. They do not find such people helpful and will not spend much time in such a relationship, nor will they commit themselves to it, unless they are desperate. To exploit the desperation of people by giving them inauthentic human contact is inexcusable.

Necessary and sufficient
One of the frequently quoted phrases from Rogers' early writings is that the six conditions are both 'necessary and sufficient' for therapeutic change to take place.

By *necessary* Rogers means that in order for therapeutic change to take place *all* of the conditions must be present. If just one condition is not present, then regardless of how much effort the counsellor puts in, therapeutic change is not possible.

By *sufficient* Rogers means that if all of the conditions are present then nothing else is required to facilitate change. Some go so far as to say that if all of the conditions are there then therapeutic change *will* take place—it is inevitable.

Many counsellors and therapists from different theoretical orientations accept the first proposition to be true, and an increasing amount of research evidence shows it to be so—it is widely acknowledged that Rogers' six conditions are necessary. Put another way, a *relationship* is the key essential ingredient in helping human distress.

On the other hand, many counsellors and therapists from different theoretical orientations *do not accept* that *all* you need in therapy are Rogers' six conditions. The majority of counsellors, as well as providing a relationship, will provide other methods and techniques as well. Such counsellors will identify themselves as practising a therapeutic approach such as 'PSYCHODYNAMIC' or 'COGNITIVE'. They might also describe themselves as 'INTEGRATIVE'; meaning that they mix together different styles and approaches to counselling, often using Rogers' conditions as a foundation, providing the relationship to which other methods are added.

However, there are person-centred counsellors who think that the six conditions are sufficient, and think that to use other techniques is unnecessary and even counter-productive. They think that the basic relationship is the healing force and everything else is a diversion, bells and whistles if you like, which might look and sound exciting, but don't actually do anything useful.

Non-directivity

Early on in his career, Rogers struggled to find a title for his approach that fully explained the ethos of his theory and method. For a brief time in the 1940s he called his approach 'Non-Directive Therapy'. This title has caused debate and controversy ever since. In Chapter 10 of the book I will look at the theory behind the idea that being non-directive is thought to be therapeutic. Here I will say a sentence or two about the controversy.

When Carl Rogers first started work as a psychologist, it usually involved listening for a while to the patient and then giving instructions or advice based on psychological theories. Rogers noticed that people seemed to have more capacity for sorting out their problems themselves than they were given credit for. Indeed he became very enthusiastic about behaving as a companion to his patients rather than an expert and he set about developing his approach as a method of facilitating self-discovery rather than the giving of advice.

This is the foundation of the idea of non-directivity and remained at the heart of his approach when he changed the name to 'client-centred'—meaning that the client was in control of the process, not the therapist. However, since then it has become a bone of contention which many see as differentiating the 'real' person-centred practice from INTEGRATIVE practice. Directing the client to talk about their feelings, rather than their thoughts, or about their family rather than their motor car, or suggesting they practice relaxation or thinking in a positive way are all signs of being an 'expert', i.e. that the therapist knows what's best for the client. Rogers thought this was not therapeutic.

Nowadays a small but increasing number of people prefer to call their practice 'Non-Directive Client-Centred Therapy' to distinguish their way of working from more INTEGRATIVE counsellors.

The differences between 'being' and 'using'

Person-centred counsellors often talk about the person-centred approach as 'a way of being'. This was the title of Rogers' last book (Rogers, 1980) and a phrase Rogers used frequently towards the end of his life. It indicates that it is better if the person-centred counsellor accepts the therapeutic conditions as a set of principles for living rather than adopts them as a set of professional practices.

In 1990, psychologist Barry Grant made an important contribution by distinguishing between types of non-directivity (see below and for more detail, Chapter 10) calling them 'instrumental' and 'principled' non-directivity. This distinction can be applied to ways of bringing the therapeutic conditions to a counselling session, and adds to our understanding of Rogers' phrase 'way of being'. We can say, for example, that the counsellor is instrumental or principled in the way that they bring the therapeutic conditions to the session.

If you use the therapeutic conditions as a tool or an instrument to further a therapeutic aim, then you are being instrumental. So if you *use* empathy in order to understand your client's problems so that you can select a counselling technique, or *use* UPR to develop trust, then you are using the conditions like tools.

On the other hand you operate in a principled fashion if you hold the conditions as principles that are fundamental to your belief system. You are not using them to gain trust or information, you are just *being* them. This is Rogers' *way of being*, and he believed that clients could tell at some level if you were putting on an act, 'being the professional' or using 'relationship technology'.

Other areas of theory

There are four other important areas of understanding in person-centred theory, namely:
- personality theory and CONDITIONS OF WORTH (Chapter 2)
- the actualising tendency (Chapter 3)
- non-directivity (Chapter 10)
- the process of change (Chapter 11)

These different components are covered in this book because it is not enough just to know *what* to do. You need to know *why* you are doing it and you need to know what is likely to happen when you do it. If counselling is based on a certain type of relationship, you need to feel confident and relaxed in yourself and what you are offering. This confidence will not come if you are 'using' counselling skills as though they were steps in a recipe or instruction manual. It is important to understand the reasons behind the things that person-centred counsellors do.

In order to be an effective counsellor you need to understand:
A. How human beings can develop into functioning adults
B. How human beings come to experience distress
C. How to get from B to A (this is therapy or counselling)

The chapters on personality, and what motivates people: the actualising tendency, give some theoretical background to (A) and (B), whilst the remainder of the book looks at the theory of therapy and its practical application.

The practice of person-centred counselling

Person-centred counselling is seen by some critics as being 'light on theory' or even simplistic. However, most agree that though it might be easy to explain the theory, it is difficult to implement it. This is my experience too, and I discovered it during counsellor training and found that there is no substitute for making a recording (audio or video) of practice counselling and receiving feedback on it from others. Throughout the book there will be plenty of examples of how the theory translates into practice and Chapter 12 contains a transcript of a counselling session and commentary on it.

When learning how to be a counsellor it can be useful to see examples of how it could be done—note 'could' not 'should'. If things get difficult in training it can be comforting to find something to anchor your understanding of good practice. It would, however, be a mistake to base your own counselling style on it.

Research into person-centred counselling

It is increasingly required that counselling approaches demonstrate the effectiveness of their 'INTERVENTIONS'. Whilst on the one hand the person-centred approach is able to do this, on the other there are several important objections to the type of evidence required. Nor are these objections just being argumentative for the sake of it—the scientific community knows full well that 'evidence' is in the eye of the beholder and the honest answer to most questions of effectiveness is 'we don't know', or 'it depends'. These issues and the evidence itself are briefly looked at in Chapter 14.

THE 'FAMILY' OF PERSON-CENTRED THERAPIES

As soon as Carl Rogers made his major theory statements in 1951, 1957 and 1959, he encouraged people to try out and test his ideas. This has led (again encouraged by Rogers) to variations and developments on his original ideas. This is the way ideas progress in science. However, it has not been a simple matter of adding bits on here and there, since Rogers' ideas are, in some ways, more than a theory of therapeutic change. Along with other theories of therapy, they are a prescription for a healthy and happy life and suddenly the stakes are much higher than if we were talking about just a psychological theory. The ideas are about values such as: all people are equal; judging people is wrong; people should be free to live their lives as they choose; people must take responsibility for their behaviour.

As new variations were proposed over the years, the debate has had two edges—first whether the new method is effective and useful and second whether the new method sticks to the values implicit in person-centred (or client-centred, as it was originally called) theory. The debates continue today, but with one important dynamic. Namely that the people proposing variations which they claim are true to, or founded in, Rogers' work are committed to working towards enhancing the 'family' of person-centred therapies, rather than splitting off into factions. In this book, for example we will learn a little about Garry Prouty's Pre-Therapy. Prouty is clear in all of his writing that he believes that his method is an evolution of Rogers' ideas. More details about variations on Rogers' ideas and the idea of a 'family' of person-centred therapies can be found in Sanders (2004). This series of *Primers* also introduces some members of the family: *Focusing-oriented counselling; Process-experiential counselling* and *Contact work*, the last one being based on Prouty's Pre-Therapy. You will find a little more on this in Chapter 4 of this book.

'Classical' client-centred counselling

Tony Merry (2002) gives a comprehensive account of 'classical' person-centred counselling and again in summary form two years later (Merry, 2004). The important features are to understand and accept the actualising tendency as the single human MOTIVATION (Chapter 3); the necessity and sufficiency of Rogers' therapeutic conditions for personality change (Chapters 4 to 9); and the inviolable sovereignty of the client and the therapeutic process demonstrated by principled non-directivity (Chapter 10).

Person-centred INTEGRATIVE counselling

Whilst several training courses advocate eclectic approaches (putting techniques from different approaches together to suit the 'diagnosis' of the client made by the counsellor), Richard Worsley describes a protocol for person-centred INTEGRATIVE counselling. Worsley (2004) advocates continuous REFLEXIVE PRACTICE which integrates all of the counsellor's life experience.

EXPERIENTIAL approaches to counselling

In the 1960s, Eugene Gendlin, a student (and later colleague) of Rogers, was interested in *how* the client changes. He concentrated on the nature of *experience* itself (hence 'EXPERIENTIAL' approaches) and developed what is now known as 'FOCUSING-oriented psychotherapy'. It stays close to Rogers' founding principles and is summarised by Campbell Purton (2004) and again in *The FOCUSING-Oriented Counselling Primer.*

Later, in the 1970s, Laura North Rice, Leslie Greenberg and Robert Elliott developed a more structured approach blending elements of Gestalt therapy with client-centred therapy and engaged on a vigorous research program to build their method on an evidence base. They called this approach 'process-EXPERIENTIAL therapy' and it is covered in more detail in *The Experiential Counselling Primer* by Nick Baker and in Baker, 2004.

DIALOGICAL (or 'encounter-oriented') approaches

Philosopher Martin Buber thought that the change process exists only in the co-created relationship between helper and 'helpee' and it has become an approach (called 'DIALOGICAL') in its own right. A DIALOGICAL approach is implicit in the recent work of Godfrey Barrett-Lennard (2005) and Dave Mearns (Mearns & Cooper, 2005), but Peter Schmid (1998, 2004) has been foremost in bringing an encounter-oriented approach to the family of person-centred therapies.

2

PERSONALITY

WHAT IS 'PERSONALITY'?

In 1937, psychologist Gordon Allport listed fifty definitions of personality (and there will be many more to list now). Personality is the relatively stable organisation of qualities, attitudes, dispositions, MOTIVATIONS and tendencies that mediate behavioural responses to the social and physical environment. Personality is what makes a person psychologically different from other people, so different that in all probability each personality is unique.

There are various sub-areas in the study of personality in traditional academic psychology, and because traditional psychology is REDUCTIONISTIC much of the study revolves around the *differences* between people's personalities. They often pay considerable attention to things like TYPES and TRAITS and PSYCHOMETRIC TESTS so that people can be categorised into personality TYPES such as 'neurotic', 'introverted' or 'extroverted'.

In everyday language, the study of personality is the study of human psychological structure—how people are *put together*, how they *work* and, of interest to counsellors, how they *fall apart*.

However, HUMANISTIC PSYCHOLOGY (of which person-centred psychology is a part) is not so interested in the differences between people as the shared commonalities—what binds us together. Carl Rogers was more interested in looking for the *essence of being a person*—what it means to be an individual human being. This is no simple task, and it means that the field of personality psychology stretches from scientific psychological exploration to a philosophical search for the meaning of life.

ROGERS' THEORY OF PERSONALITY

Carl Rogers made his first attempt at a comprehensive theory of personality in Chapter 11 of his 1951 book *Client-Centered Therapy* (see Chapter 1, p. 6, this volume). He arranged his ideas into nineteen propositions (theoretical statements) about human psychological development, the nature of human mental life, the structure of personality, how this structure can be prone to weaknesses, the nature of psychological distress, and how distress can be put right. In his major 1959 writing (see Chapter 1, p. 7, this volume), Rogers included a refinement of this personality theory.

In the preceding paragraph, I have been deliberately colloquial and rather relaxed in my use of words, since at this stage in this book, I am trying to explain general principles. Later you will discover that I will better explain and fine-tune some of these phrases so that they are more in accord with person-centred theory.

Rogers divided the theory into eight sections (Rogers, 1959) and what follows is a summary (including elements from Rogers' 1951 writing) with the psychological jargon removed. However, readers who intend to progress to diploma-level training are directed to any version of Rogers' original material for the full details.

The human infant, their development and their needs
- The infant experiences herself as the centre of 'reality', i.e. the ever-changing world around her.
- For the infant, this experience *is* reality.
- The infant has an inherent tendency to actualise, maintain and enhance itself (actualising tendency, Chapter 3).
- The infant responds to her world (reality-as-experienced) in an organised way as a whole organism, as a result of the needs she experiences in order to actualise.
- The infant has an inherent tendency to value experiences which maintain and enhance its organism positively. Experiences which work against actualisation of the organism are valued negatively. 'Valuing' can mean something as simple as 'liking' or 'enjoying'. This is the ORGANISMIC VALUING PROCESS.
- The infant is attracted towards and accepts positively valued experiences (those it likes) whilst avoiding and rejecting negatively valued experiences (those it doesn't like).

> **Illustrative example**: *As he explores his world, 'X' discovers that he is attracted to other boys and sexually aroused in the presence of other boys. This is the result of his tendency to actualise and his* ORGANISMIC VALUING PROCESS. *Because he likes this experience, he seeks the company of boys.*

The development of personality

- As development proceeds, at some point the infant differentiates a part of their world-as-experienced as having a particular quality; being different and 'special'. This differentiated portion of experiences comes into awareness as the *self*.

- The infant builds up a picture of itself as it experiences the world, particularly as a result of being with others and being evaluated by others. This picture is the SELF-CONCEPT.

- As the infant becomes aware of its *self*, its general need for satisfaction (originating in the acceptance of actualising experiences) becomes a particular need for *positive regard* from others.

- Positive regard from others is so potent (because it is associated with enhancement of the actualising organism) that it becomes more compelling than the ORGANISMIC VALUING PROCESS in determining behaviour.

- Such evaluations from others are taken into the self-concept as though they had originated from the ORGANISMIC VALUING PROCESS and are called INTROJECTED VALUES.

- When the infant accepts or avoids a self-experience as a result of positive regard from another, the infant has developed a CONDITION OF WORTH.

- As the self develops into a recognisable entity, it too has a tendency to actualise—to maintain and enhance itself (self-actualisation, see Chapter 3, pp. 30–32). But because the self may contain material INTROJECTED directly from the evaluations of others, the self may actualise in a different direction to that of the organism.

- This is a state of disharmony between self and organism.

- The individual awareness tends to be dominated by self-related experience. In other words, the self becomes the focus of attention, through which all experience is processed. So it is important that experiences can be recognised and handled by the SELF-STRUCTURE.

Illustrative example: *As 'X' continues to explore his world, he finds that his parents discourage his interest in boys to the point of letting him know in no uncertain terms that no son of theirs should behave in that way. Over time, 'X' begins to accept that his interest in boys is 'improper' and he takes this into his self-concept. His SELF-CONCEPT now contains an INTROJECTED value that, as a boy he will not be attracted to, nor aroused by other boys. His SELF-CONCEPT is energised through self-actualisation, which is now at odds with his organism as a whole.*

Congruence/incongruence—and PSYCHOLOGICAL TENSION

- When the individual has an experience which fits with its SELF-CONCEPT, the experience is in harmony, or congruent with its SELF-STRUCTURE and can be SYMBOLISED accurately.
- However, since the SELF-CONCEPT contains INTROJECTED material, the individual will have experiences which are not in harmony with its SELF-STRUCTURE and may not be SYMBOLISED accurately. This is incongruence between self and experience. This leads to PSYCHOLOGICAL TENSION.
- The more disharmony there is between self and the organism as a result of INTROJECTS, the greater is the likelihood of incongruence between self and experience, and a greater potential for PSYCHOLOGICAL TENSION.
- As there is incongruence between self and experience, so incongruence also develops between two sorts of behaviour:
  - behaviours consistent with the SELF-CONCEPT *(the individual is aware of this behaviour)* and
  - behaviours consistent with the rest of the organism *(the individual may not recognise these behaviours as self-related, i.e. may not 'own' them).*

Illustrative example: *'X' grows up and continues to accept that as a boy (his SELF-CONCEPT) he is not attracted to other boys. However,*

> *the remainder of him, the rest of his organism as it also has a tendency to actualise, continues to have feelings of arousal in the presence of other boys. 'X' is confused and upset by these feelings on the few occasions they break through into awareness.*

Threat, defence, breakdown and therapeutic change

- Experiences which are incongruent with the self not only may not be SYMBOLISED accurately, but they are also experienced as threatening to the integrity of the self. The experiences would imply that the SELF-CONCEPT was 'wrong', and since this is the effective centre of the SELF-STRUCTURE, the whole of the self would be under threat.
- Threatening experiences are dealt with in two sorts of ways:
  - *they can fail to come into full awareness (they are DENIED SYMBOLISATION to experience).*
  - *they can be changed so that they fit (DISTORTED) into the SELF-CONCEPT without threat.*

> **Illustrative example**: *'X' is determined to be a good son and most of the time isn't aware of how attracted he is to boys. He convinces himself that the occasional feelings of arousal he is aware of are the 'natural growing feelings' he has read about in books. Encouraged by his parents, who are desperate for grandchildren, 'X' marries a woman he has known since childhood.*

- In a healthy individual the SELF-CONCEPT is a changing, flexible collection of ideas about 'me' or 'I'. When it is under threat though, the organism protects itself further by making the SELF-CONCEPT rigid and inflexible. As it becomes more rigid it relies on past experiences and so more and more current experiences will be DISTORTED or DENIED.
- The processes of defence become entrenched and PSYCHOLOGICAL TENSION builds up so that under certain circumstances (a particularly large threat to the SELF-CONCEPT, or the accumulation of threat), the SELF-CONCEPT effectively 'breaks' under the pressure. The resulting state of disorganisation will be experienced idiosyncratically by the

individual as anxiety, depression, confusion, pain, or colloquially, a 'nervous breakdown'.

Illustrative example: *'X' is talking to an attractive, effeminate man at a party and it gradually dawns on him that he is flirting with the man. At first he puts it down to the fact that the man looks and behaves in a feminine way and reasons that any red-blooded male would fancy him. After the party his wife, who feels that 'X' is not interested in her sexually, challenges 'X' about his apparent flirting with the man at the party. Confused, upset and feeling he has to please people on all sides, he is completely overwhelmed by turbulent feelings and has a 'panic attack'. His GP refers him to the practice counsellor.*

• The organism will be restored by integration of all experiences into the SELF-CONCEPT. However, the SELF-CONCEPT will continue to resist this by DENIAL and DISTORTION. Removing threat to the SELF-CONCEPT will result in a relaxation of its rigidity and its defences. Newer experiences, previously discrepant with the SELF-CONCEPT may be tentatively admitted and the process of integration begins. This is the process of therapeutic change.

CHARACTERISTICS OF PERSON-CENTRED PERSONALITY THEORY

It is interesting to note the characteristics of person-centred personality theory in the sense that is different from other theories of the era. This may help you make better comparisons for your own understanding, assignments or discussions with other practitioners. The following terms have been used in various places to explain and describe Rogers' theory.

A PHENOMENOLOGICAL theory

PHENOMENOLOGY is a philosophical position which states that understanding of 'reality' comes from subjective experience. In the context of personality theory, a PHENOMENOLOGICAL position is one where we think that the 'truth' about experience is generated within the individual, not something that has to be or can ever be validated by 'objective' observers.

So a PHENOMENOLOGICAL theory would be about '*my* truth in *my* world of experience' not '*the* truth in *the* world' not 'what exists' but 'what *I believe* exists'. This would be important in distinguishing person-centred theory from a positivist theory like BEHAVIOURISM, which has it that the only valid experience is one that can be observed and measured.

It is doubtful that Carl Rogers read any of the works of philosopher Edmund Husserl who founded PHENOMENOLOGY around the 1850s, yet the first two propositions (Rogers, 1951: 483–4) clearly locate his personality theory as PHENOMENOLOGICAL:

I) Every individual exists in a continually changing world of experience of which he is the center.

II) The organism reacts to the field as it is experienced and perceived. This perceptual field is, for the individual, 'reality'.

The PHENOMENOLOGICAL nature of the theory has important consequences in that it puts empathy at the centre of understanding the world of the client, not external observation, measurement and expert analysis (see Chapter 8). The counsellor must be unprejudiced and 'naïve' when they encounter the client's world.

A perceptual theory

Closely related to PHENOMENOLOGY is the fact that some theories of personality are based on the idea that behaviour is changed as a result of changing *perception*. Since the client's reality is based on their perception of the world, then a change in perception leads to a change in experience and behaviour. Combs and Snygg (1959) state:

All behaviour, without exception, is completely determined by, and pertinent to, the perceptual field of the behaving organism … By the perceptual field, we mean the entire universe, including himself, as it is experienced by the individual … (p. 20)

What we must remember is that reality-as-experienced is different for everyone—the sum total of how each individual person's different histories, needs and expectations affects their perceptions in the moment. The client is, therefore, the expert; not the counsellor. In the 1950s, this was a radical idea.

A HUMANISTIC theory

Corliss Lamont, a leading proponent of modern humanism defines it as 'a naturalistic philosophy that rejects all supernaturalism and relies primarily upon reason and science, democracy and human compassion'. It is important to understand the humanist foundations of Rogers' theory since it rejected certain culturally embedded notions of the era. In particular Rogers promoted the idea that humans were responsible for (and therefore could influence) the human condition. From mental health through to the politics of conflict resolution, Rogers believed that human relationships were the active factor in promoting positive growth and change.

Popular at the time was Freudian theory, which some believe echoed ideas of original sin, or 'the fall from grace', suggesting that humans were inherently, essentially and inevitably evil, flawed or driven by self- and other-destructive urges. Rogers was keen to present a radically different and positive view of human nature in which humans were indeed responsible for evil behaviour, but not because of an *inherent* flaw or 'dark' or 'SHADOW' side. He dismissed such ideas with statements such as:

> If I endeavored to explain to you that if the 'lion-ness' of the lion were to be released, or the 'sheep-ness' of the sheep, that these animals would then be impelled by insatiable lusts, uncontrollable aggressions, wild and excessive sexual behaviors, and tendencies of innate destructiveness, you would quite properly laugh at me. Obviously, such a view is pure nonsense.
>
> ... I find that man, like the lion, has a nature. My experience is that he is a basically trustworthy member of the human species, whose deepest characteristics tend toward development, differentiation, co-operative relationships; whose life tends fundamentally to move from dependence to independence; whose impulses tend naturally to harmonise into a complex and changing pattern of self-regulation; whose total character is such as to tend to preserve and enhance himself and his species, and perhaps to move it toward its further evolution. (Rogers, 1957, reprinted in Kirschenbaum & Henderson, 1989: 404–5)

A holistic theory

Holism is the idea that a complex system (like a human being) is more than the sum of its parts, and that in order to understand it, the whole organism must be studied as one. Readers will probably be familiar with the term *holistic medicine*, i.e. the idea that the whole person, including psychological, social *and* physical factors, needs to be taken into account, rather than treating just the physical symptoms of a disease.

Rogers' theory was holistic before holism was fashionable. In 1951 he wrote the first of a series of statements which clearly indicate his recognition that you cannot understand a human organism by breaking it up into its constituent parts (REDUCTIONISM):

> [Proposition] III) The organism reacts as an organized whole to this PHENOMENAL field. (Rogers, 1951: 486)

A fulfilment of potential, growth-oriented theory

Readers will be aware of the obvious fact that this book is about 'client-' or 'person-'centred counselling, but in addition, throughout the book (e.g. Chapter 5) you will notice that Rogers' theory is a growth-oriented theory. This means that the person-centred metaphor for recovery is not one of 'cure' (of an 'illness'), or one of 'mending' (something that is broken), or even one of 'reprogramming' or 'debugging' a set of instructions. The person-centred metaphor for recovery is one of growth or development to a new way of being. Although the personality theory gives us an account of how things can go wrong, it focuses on fulfilment of potential. This is very different from other theories.

A process theory

I could have said 'new *state* of being' a few lines above. However, another radical characteristic of Rogers' personality theory is that over the years (although it didn't technically start out this way), it has become a theory where personality is not a 'thing', but a 'process'; nor is the self a thing, and indeed, personhood, or being human, is a 'process', not a 'state'. This is covered in more detail in Chapter 11.

3

THE ACTUALISING TENDENCY

This chapter looks at the area of MOTIVATION, or in terms of person-centred theory, 'the actualising tendency'. Readers with a background in psychology will be au fait with MOTIVATION, although they might not have come across Rogers' idea of the actualising tendency. Other readers will probably not be surprised to learn that there is a good deal of debate on the subject of what causes us to behave in the ways we do.

Whether you are a social scientist by training or not, you will be concerned with the idea of MOTIVATION. MOTIVATION is the term used by psychologists to describe the study of why people do things, (or more correctly, *what makes animals do things*) and so after a moment's thought it is clear why it is central to our understanding of distress, change and fulfilment. It may come as no surprise to discover that there are many competing theories as to what 'makes' us do things and there is hardly any actual 'evidence' that any of these theories is correct.

Traditionally, in an effort to understand why animals exhibit any behaviour at all, psychologists start with the obvious behaviours that seem connected to survival of the individual and the species regarding eating, drinking, pain avoidance and reproducing. Behaviour related to these survival needs seems to be the most simple and straightforward to study. The biological energies pushing us to meet these needs are routinely called 'DRIVES' by psychologists, and theories built around these DRIVES are called 'DRIVE theories'. DRIVE theories are based on the concept of 'HOMOEOSTASIS', i.e. maintaining a steady state with regard to a physiological need (the DRIVES to survive: to eat, drink, and avoid pain are called 'primary DRIVES'). So when the organism doesn't have enough nutrients, its behaviour becomes directed towards the goal of getting food and eating. Or when its body fluids get out of balance, its behaviour becomes directed towards finding water and drinking. A corollary of this idea is that behaviour only happens when there is some kind of primary internal need, i.e. for food, water, sex or pain avoidance. The problem is that even when an organism's primary needs are met, it is awake and active.

More apparently complicated behaviour is very much more difficult to understand. One way of trying to understand the MOTIVATION behind complex behaviour is to try to tie everything back to physiological DRIVES. Examples of DRIVE theories which have an impact on counselling are Freudian PSYCHOANALYSIS and BEHAVIOURISM.

HUMANISTIC PSYCHOLOGY AND MOTIVATION

HUMANISTIC psychology tends to be more holistic than either PSYCHOANALYSIS or BEHAVIOURISM and so isn't in favour of reducing complex human behaviour to what its advocates would consider to be over-simplistic DRIVES. Abraham Maslow (1954) argued that human behaviour was much more complicated than could be accounted for by physiological HOMOEOSTASIS. Rather than propose a simple deficit-DRIVE-satiation model (i.e. lack nutrients–feel hunger–seek food–and eat–model), Maslow proposed a wide range of human needs in a dynamic and changing system. He suggested a hierarchy of needs, where needs at higher levels would only be addressed when needs at lower levels had been satisfied (see Figure 1 below). It is important to note that Maslow uses the term self-actualisation differently from the way Rogers uses it.

THE ACTUALISING TENDENCY

Splitting behaviour up into categories according to different DRIVES, and so having categories of MOTIVATION, seemed irrelevant to Rogers. Person-centred psychology subscribes wholeheartedly to the single idea that an organism always strives to maintain and enhance itself in everything it does. This is what Rogers called the actualising tendency. It is what living organisms do.

Having made such an apparently simple and bold statement,

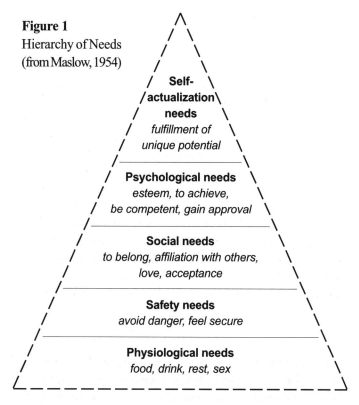

Figure 1
Hierarchy of Needs
(from Maslow, 1954)

Self-actualization needs
fulfillment of unique potential

Psychological needs
esteem, to achieve, be competent, gain approval

Social needs
to belong, affiliation with others, love, acceptance

Safety needs
avoid danger, feel secure

Physiological needs
food, drink, rest, sex

we need to look at what this might mean in a little more detail. First, it is the tendency of the organism to express itself in a number of domains, so at a basic level it is the biological actuality of the organism becoming itself. It is also the story, so to speak, of how the organism becomes a unique example of its species. Second, as a concept it puts crucial distance between person-centred and PSYCHOANALYTIC psychologies. There are no 'hidden' DRIVES in the tendency to actualise, nor can it hold any inbuilt self-destructive DRIVES, no 'DEATH INSTINCT' or 'SHADOW SIDE'. As Rogers said:

> I can sense the reactions of some of my readers … 'Do you mean that man [sic] [is] nothing but a human *organism* …? Who will control him? Who will SOCIALISE him? … Have you merely released the id in man?' To which the most adequate reply seems to be … 'He is realistically able to control himself and he is incorrigibly

socialized in his desires. There is no beast in man. There is only man in man.' (Rogers, 1961: 105, original emphasis)

Barrett-Lennard (1998: 74–6) explains that the actualising tendency is then *inherent,* i.e. it is built in to the organism; a quality of life itself. It is also *active* in that it doesn't wait for a deficit in something in order to maintain HOMOEOSTASIS; it is present and operating continuously. Third, the actualising tendency is *directional* in that the organism inexorably moves towards development, enhancement, differentiation and increasing complexity. Fourth, contrary to the DRIVE-reduction mechanisms in other theories of MOTIVATION, the actualising tendency *increases tension* in the organism, making it continually strive for new experiences. It can never be satisfied. This leads to an organism in continuous motion; a motion evident and integrated from its continuous flow of experience through to its complex social behaviour and creativity (see also Embleton Tudor, Keemar, et al., 2004: 26–31).

During development in infancy and childhood, however, the actualising tendency becomes shaped by SOCIALISATION (the rules and regulations of living as a human being in the company of others). This will be looked at in more detail in Chapter 11 and for now we need no more than a sketch of how the process of development might, for want of a better term, 'go wrong'. It is easy to see how the actualising tendency can be crudely portrayed as the individual organism growing into health, or healing itself if the right conditions prevail. This is the fundamental position of person-centred therapy; when the actualising tendency is unfettered by restrictions the organism flourishes and may realise its full potential. In the right conditions, the individual may become in Rogers' terms 'fully functioning' (Rogers, 1959), and be psychologically well-adjusted. We have seen in Chapter 1 what these 'right conditions' are which will lead to fulfilment of potential, therapeutic change and psychological adjustment. This is Rogers' simple 'if–then' hypothesis (*if* the conditions are provided, *then* the organism will heal) and it is based on the tendency inherent in the organism to actualise itself.

The question is, 'How, if the tendency is for the organism to grow towards health, does the organism come to grow towards maladjustment, anxiety, vulnerability and distress?' The answer is that the psychological and material environments in which the vast majority of the human race are reared are somewhat less than ideal (see Merry, 1995). Roughly speaking, Rogers' ideal psychological environment for therapeutic change translates into the ideal environment for child-rearing; namely an environment free from fear and judgement, one rich in understanding, and authentic unconditional love. Such environments are not commonplace.

Individual or community?

The *person*-centred approach champions the individual organism. The clue, as they say, is in the title. Critics of person-centred theory frequently alight upon the elements of the actualising tendency which appear to advance the individual at the expense of others and social relations. Rampant INDIVIDUALISM is not an attractive trait and we could be forgiven for expecting a fully actualised *individual* to be selfish. What provision is there in the actualising tendency concept for the maintenance and enhancement of the human organism as a social animal? Before you come to a conclusion yourself, you will also need to read the next section on 'self-actualisation'.

Rogers' writings regarding a 'fully functioning' person are peppered with references to SOCIALISATION, self-regulation, living in harmony with others, and community. The quote taken from Rogers (1961) above (page 27–8) is but one example of many I could take to illustrate this point. What is important here is that the fully functioning person is the product of the actualising tendency. It is the direction in which the actualising tendency is pointing. According to Rogers the fully functioning person is 'soundly and realistically social' (1961: 192).

One problem is that even though SOCIALISATION is the natural consequence of social living and parenting, it is sometimes portrayed as being antagonistic towards, or set against, the natural development of the individual in person-centred theory. It is true to say that the individualist theme of the actualising tendency has been taken by some to show how the concept can be aligned with late capitalist Western INDIVIDUALISM. It is also true to say that Rogers did not intend it to be taken that way (see Rogers, 1980).

Of the modern person-centred theorists, Mearns and Thorne have done most to elaborate the possible social dimensions of the actualising tendency. They introduced the idea of a creative tension between the actualising tendency and the social environment as a positive developmental energy (Mearns & Thorne, 2000: 173–89). This idea is elegantly simple and instructive. First, it suggests that we look again at the significance of social and material contexts in the development of persons. Second, it reminds us that the actualising tendency must have pro-social elements in a social animal. Third, it asserts that the actualising tendency is multidirectional in its efforts to enhance the organism—it could equally energise change as it could energise resistance to change, i.e. the organism might sense that change isn't always good and might resist change in order to survive and be enhanced. Finally, Mearns and Thorne remind us that the pivot of the actualising tendency is the experience of the individual—not isolated, but as a social being in many social contexts.

What does all this mean? In essence, that in the twenty-first century it would be inaccurate to characterise the actualising tendency as an excuse for Western INDIVIDUALISM. Person-centred theory sees the 'sole MOTIVATIONAL force' of the human organism as enhancing the *connected individual-in-context*, not the *isolated individual ruthlessly pursuing its own interests against all else*.

SELF-ACTUALISATION

Part of the natural developmental process of becoming a human adult involves the development of a 'self', i.e. developing an idea of 'me' or 'I', separate from my experience of the rest of the world. Since our 'psychological life' is a natural element of being human, it is actualised along with everything else—our existence as thinking, feeling beings is maintained and developed as a part of living. Rogers believed that the maintenance and development of the 'self' component of human psychology is also a natural fact of humanness.

Rogers' proposition that a sense of self develops as the infant grows, puts person-centred theory clearly in the 'SELF-PSYCHOLOGY' tradition and has recently been questioned from a number of quarters. Many of the arguments against SELF-PSYCHOLOGY are too complicated to consider in any detail here, but one is fairly straightforward, namely that the idea of 'self' is a uniquely Western one and probably not held by the majority of people on the planet. In other words it is a culturally embedded ethnocentric concept. If person-centred psychology claims to have universal applicability, it must avoid such culturally specific concepts.

Nevertheless, when a person *does* experience this sense of self (whether as a result of SOCIALISATION or not) it will be actualised, and the term 'self-actualisation' refers to the actualisation of this particular element of our experience. This presents us with a conundrum which we started to look at in the previous section. We can see that on the one hand the organism itself can actualise as a whole entity in a positive, constructive way that fits a social species. On the other hand we can also see that once the self emerges, it might actualise in the direction of survival and enhancement of the SELF-STRUCTURE rather than the organism as a whole. Moreover, *self*-actualisation can often be in a different, possibly antagonistic direction from the pro-social organismic actualising tendency of the whole organism.

This can happen when the self contains many INTROJECTED CONDITIONS OF WORTH (see Chapters 4 and 12). For example a young girl, punished for playing with 'masculine' toys, and 'told' that she is only lovable if she behaves 'like a proper little girl', will INTROJECT the idea that she loves pink frilly dresses and dolls. Here we have the potential for tension between the tendency of (a) the organism to actualise in the direction of pleasurable exploration of *all* toys and experiences, and (b) the self to actualise in the direction of the INTROJECTED CONDITIONS OF WORTH, i.e. to explore and enjoy only those gendered objects and experiences approved by her parents.

Understanding this split between the actualising tendency and self-actualisation is one of the foundations of person-centred counselling theory. If the material, social and psychological conditions during development are favourable, then the organism and self actualise in tandem towards full-functioning of the organism's potential. If the conditions are not favourable, then these two elements may diverge and actualisation of the self can be potentially set against the actualisation of the organism as a whole. Rogers suggested that the psychological environment becomes unfavourable when the individual only feels loved when s/he conforms to certain expectations, and he called this effect 'CONDITIONS OF WORTH'. So, in our efforts to experience love, the development of our 'self' can be set against the development of the rest of our organism. PSYCHOLOGICAL TENSION is now much more likely, or even inevitable. This tension can be rectified by adjusting the living conditions of the organism. How should the conditions be adjusted? On a material and social level, by providing a safe and secure environment free from physical need, and on a psychological level by following Rogers' recipe of necessary and sufficient conditions for therapeutic change. The organism and self are then potentially able to actualise in harmony.

THE FORMATIVE TENDENCY

Later in his life Rogers (1980) came to understand the actualising tendency in human beings as part of a more universal force at work in the universe—a tendency which moved everything to become itself. This applied to all physical matter, animate or inanimate, from single-celled creatures to the formation of stars and galaxies. He called this the *formative tendency*.

For some observers, the concept of the formative tendency was a sign that Rogers had overreached the limits of psychotherapy. For others it was evidence that Rogers was trying to put human MOTIVATION, development and healing in a bigger context. In his later years in California he had discussions with philosophers and Nobel prize-winning quantum physicists. These discussions led him to see human psychology, distress and its healing as in accord with larger systems of order in nature and the universe.

4

PSYCHOLOGICAL CONTACT (CONDITION 1)

WHAT ROGERS HAD TO SAY

Carl Rogers' first condition is one that has been consistently overlooked in most books on counselling. It is also overlooked on some counselling courses and many counsellors do not spend much time thinking about it either. Psychological contact, according to Rogers, must exist between the counsellor and the client before anything else can happen. Rogers thought that this first condition could be more-or-less assumed. If two people were in the same room and looking at each other, then psychological contact could be said to exist.

It is clear that in the 1950s it was very much against the run of psychological ideas to suggest that the relationship between the counsellor and client was important. Yet this was exactly Rogers' point:

> The first condition specifies that a minimum relationship ... must exist. I am hypothesizing that significant positive personality change does not occur except in a relationship. (Rogers, 1957, quoted in Kirschenbaum & Henderson, 1990: 221)

Rogers wrote little else about this therapeutic condition because he thought it was so simple and obvious. It patently seemed thus to most other theorists as well and so psychological contact remained under-studied for decades. Yet to assert so clearly that the relationship is the essential foundation of therapy was a clear and radical statement then and remains so today. Furthermore, 'the relationship' is not seen as an object external to the client and counsellor (in the sense of three things being in the therapy room: the client, the counsellor and the relationship). The relationship *is* the client and counsellor. They do not bring 'elements' or 'things' to their time together, they bring themselves, and the unique and ever-changing relationship is the result.

In person-centred psychology, human beings are understood to be social animals. We are adapted to be relational beings and healing distress is one of the many human events that appears to require connection with another human being.

HUMAN-TO-HUMAN CONTACT

Psychologists have discovered a fair amount about contact between animals that live in social groups. For example, in 1959 American psychologist Harry Harlow discovered that monkeys denied physical and emotional contact during infancy grew up psychologically and physically damaged. He discovered that infant monkeys preferred a cuddly surrogate mother to one less cuddly but with food. He called this *contact comfort*. He even noticed that the baby monkeys were more confident simply in the presence of the more cuddly mother, even when they weren't touching it (Harlow, 1959).

Interestingly, Mary Carlson, associate professor of neuroscience and psychology at Harvard Medical School, one of Harlow's students, travelled to Romania after the fall of Ceausescu to discover that the children reared in similar circumstances to Harlow's monkeys grew up with comparable permanent behavioural and emotional problems. She confirmed that in order to be human we need to grow in an interactive human environment.

Margaret Warner believes that we are built to expect the 'meaningful presence' of other human beings and 'tend to feel intense discomfort when [we] are unable to achieve it' (Warner, 2002: 81). She also looked at the course of human development, and suggested that psychological contact was essential in the determination of healthy adult personality.

John Bowlby, a PSYCHODYNAMIC psychologist working with children separated from their mothers in infancy showed that human beings deprived of affection and the opportunity to bond with a caretaker grow up damaged (Bowlby, 1953).

Human beings cannot survive without contact. An out-of-contact person, an isolated person, will become PSYCHOTIC and soon die. Humans subjected to solitary confinement or sensory deprivation rarely survive intact. In short we can say without fear of contradiction that human-to-human contact is both essential to healthy development and essential to healthy functioning.

PSYCHOLOGICAL CONTACT

If contact with others is so important for the development and growth of healthy personality, it is hardly surprising that psychological contact, or 'relationship' (Rogers, 1957; Gaylin, 2001) or 'meaningful presence' (Warner, 2002) is implicated in successful therapy.

Client-centred theorist and commentator Shlien (1961), remarking on the nature of psychological contact, suggested that the human mind requires another before it can function as a human mind at all. He explained that:

> The mind emerges through a process of communication. This involves social interaction on the basis of what Mead calls 'significant symbols' (usually words). A significant symbol is one that is 'reflexive', i.e. when it is used it *presupposes another* person … *Acknowledging the other is essential to the existence of mind*, from beginning to end. (p. 296, original emphasis)

And, more related to the therapeutic situation, he also recollected:

> Two colleagues have described to me their reaction to a hallucinogenic drug. Both were deeply shaken, both terrified by the sense of 'not being', and significantly, both wanted above all to have human contact with a person, or persons, who *must not leave*. (p. 294, original emphasis)

Similar experiences of secure safety and comfort through contact with another can be found in just about everyone's experience at one time or another in their life. Of course person-centred theorists are not the only ones nor the first to locate contact at the centre of human psychology. To reiterate Whelton and Greenberg's declaration of the obvious: 'The type of contact that is called 'psychological' is the type of contact that a human self has with another human self' (Whelton & Greenberg, 2002: 107). They are simply stating, along with countless others, that contact brings selves together because self requires self, self begets self and self heals self. Contact between persons is the most basic, most fundamental dynamic of humanity.

What is psychological contact?

This is a fairly new and unusual question to ask. The many assumptions are quickly revealed when we run out of ideas beyond muttering something about eye contact. To acknowledge the fledgling state of our understanding of this connection, I prefer to ask a series of further related questions which reveal the possibilities for complexity.

• Is psychological contact an all-or-nothing phenomenon, or are there levels of contact?

One of the first elements of contact to consider is whether it is a binary, all-or-nothing, on–off event, or whether there are levels of psychological contact. Rogers clearly thought that it is an all-or-nothing affair, a position held today by Embleton Tudor, Keemar, et al., (2004). Others argue that there are levels of contact; see Cameron (2004) and later in this chapter.

• What are the signs of psychological contact? How do you know you are in psychological contact with another person?

The following qualities are worth considering: that there is recognition between two people of each other's presence and that they are responsive and show understanding.

• What are the minimum requirements for psychological contact?

What are the necessary sensory cues? Can psychological contact be established and maintained by telephone, by email?[1]

---

1. Murphy and Mitchell (1998) reported a client writing the following note to their counsellor after 'email counselling': 'In just our brief exchange of messages you have left me with a sense that you are a caring, creative, helpful, hopeful soul. This is hard to achieve in person, let alone in the imperfect world of electronic communication. Your warmth and humanity shine through the pixels on my screen, and come at a time when I need them most. For this I thank you and congratulate you. The irony is not lost on me that I find a true person in the virtual void at the same time as a doctor in my home county has given me short shrift' (p. 23). This is an indication of

There are further dimensions of contact, of particular concern to therapists, which could be understood as the *length* and *breadth* of contact. What do we mean by this? In short, we mean the time spent in contact with a client and the range of contact activities.

Psychological contact in the service of therapy does not have to be limited to 50-minute sessions. Several therapeutic settings involve shorter and longer time periods. Some very vulnerable clients can only tolerate short periods of contact whilst group therapy and residential therapeutic communities provide opportunities for good psychological contact over extended periods of time.

Also, there is nothing to suggest that the only effective therapeutic activity is talking in a conversational manner. Psychodrama, creative arts approaches, and occupational therapy all show us that psychological contact can be established and maintained through painting, sculpting, movement, drama, gardening, praying together, and a multitude of other activities.

New thinking about psychological contact
Rose Cameron, an articulate advocate of the notion of levels of contact recently wrote:

> The importance of this [psychological contact] in counselling is, as Rogers says, so obvious that it hardly needs mentioning. What is very much worth mentioning, however, is that there are different degrees of psychological contact. The depth of contact is what makes the difference between a rather mechanical and lifeless therapeutic relationship and one that shimmers with energy and involvement. (Cameron, 2004: 87)

She goes on to describe and name four levels of psychological contact: basic, COGNITIVE, emotional and subtle. These terms relate to the fundamental coordinates of relating: meeting (basic), understanding (COGNITIVE), emotional closeness and what she calls intimacy or 'subtle' contact (which Thorne might call 'tenderness'

---

computer-mediated psychological contact, since, according to person-centred theory, contact *has* to be made before therapeutic change can take place.

(1985/1991)) and Rogers (in Kirschenbaum & Henderson, 1990: 137, 'presence'—see page 42, this volume).

She makes further assertions regarding the nature of contact, some elaborations of Rogers' idea, some excursions into newer theoretical territory, for example: that contact is mutual (is it reciprocal?); that contact is consensual, i.e. both parties must give permission for contact, or must choose contact. Therefore we are not indiscriminately available for contact. People can and do put limits on psychological contact. Davies and Ayckroyd (2002) for example, show how members of oppressed groups deliberately hold themselves out of contact in order to protect themselves.

PRE-THERAPY: REACHING CONTACT-IMPAIRED CLIENTS

In the 1970s, American psychologist Garry Prouty turned the spotlight on Rogers' first condition with his work on *pre-therapy* (Prouty, Van Werde & Pörtner, 2002). Pre-therapy is a new way of working with people who cannot make psychological contact due to PSYCHOSIS, severe and pervasive learning disability, dementia and Alzheimer's disease, or brain damage through ORGANIC DISEASE or injury. It is a huge understatement to say that pre-therapy appears simple to describe but turns out to be difficult to do, so I recommend further reading and specific experience of a pre-therapy workshop.

Contact functions and reflections

Pre-therapy as a method is deceptively simple. In practical terms it is a continual re-presentation of elements of shared reality, or as Prouty says it 'points at the concrete', encouraging contact with self, the world and others. The elements of pre-therapy are:

- Contact Functions (the client's process)
- Contact Reflections (the therapist's responses)
- Contact Behaviours (the client's behaviour)

Contact Functions
- Reality Contact (awareness of the 'world', specifically people, places, things and events)

- Affective Contact (awareness of moods, feelings and emotions)
- Communicative Contact (SYMBOLISATION of world and affect to others—using words or sentences)

Contact Reflections
- Situational Reflections (SR) Reflecting aspects of the shared environment
- Facial Reflections (FR) Reflecting verbally or by 'mimicking' the facial expressions of the client
- Body Reflections (BR) Reflecting, verbally or posturally, the gestures, movement and postures of the client
- Word-for-Word Reflections (WWR) Repeating back what the client says word for word
- Reiterative Reflections (RR) Remaking contact by repetition of previous reflections that showed an effect

It is worth repeating that although pre-therapy is easy to describe, it is difficult to get across the subtlety of observation, pace and timing required. When addressing counsellors and therapists, Prouty says that pre-therapy requires a shift from listening to looking. The therapist must pay attention to the slightest changes in the client's behaviour: breathing, eye movements, muscle tension, variations in posture or repetitive movements, etc. Changes in contact are more often than not signalled by non-verbal contact behaviours.

Pre-therapy, contact work and a 'contact milieu'
Garry Prouty and his associates are concerned to explain the differences between *pre-therapy proper*, *contact work* and a *'contact milieu'*. These are different applications of Prouty's contact reflections.

Pre-therapy refers to work with clients who have severe and enduring mental health problems (usually a diagnosis of SCHIZOPHRENIA, possibly with other complications) or a severe and pervasive learning or communication disability (including any due to accident or illness). Such clients are chronically withdrawn and incommunicative. In these circumstances the pre-therapy effort will take weeks or months of regular sessions (some sessions may be several hours long) before any sign of improvement is evident. Marked improvement can take many months or years. See Prouty, Van Werde and Pörtner, 2002 for examples.

Contact work is a term describing the use of contact reflections with clients who may have a diagnosis of an enduring PSYCHOTIC condition, but whose contact functions are variable. In other words they move in and out of contact in quite a short period of time, e.g. a few minutes. Contact work can be done in everyday settings to enhance a person's day-to-day care. Dion Van Werde describes contact work in what he terms the *grey zone*, i.e. the zone of functioning between PSYCHOTIC functioning and normal functioning; where a person slips repeatedly between being in contact and out of contact (see Prouty, Van Werde & Pörtner, 2002).

Increased attention to psychological contact and the efficacy of contact reflections has excited interest in the application of contact work in an increasingly wide range of settings:

- Dissociative states—where people have periods of 'absence', common in post-trauma conditions—see Coffeng, 2002.
- Dementia—when people increasingly lose contact with shared reality—see Van Werde & Morton, 1999.
- Palliative care—increasing communicative contact with patients with terminal conditions helps day-to-day care and pain control.

A *contact milieu* is any setting which is permanently and pervasively oriented towards psychological contact. The term 'contact milieu' is usually applied to care settings where all staff (all professional staff, nursing staff and ancillary staff) are trained in using contact reflections. Whilst contact work is effective in facilitating one-to-one communication in the here and now, it is even more effective when it permeates the ward or institutional milieu. When an all-embracing contact milieu is established, all aspects of care are made easier, more effective and more rewarding, being effective in situations where high levels of agitation, confusion and distress are debilitating for staff and contribute to a high-stress environment.

The effects of contact reflections

Restoring an out-of-contact person to full contact has obvious benefits; in particular it allows emotional expression to develop—an important precursor to therapeutic change in any approach that builds a WORKING ALLIANCE. But it is not only a basic component of pre-therapeutic work (i.e. it helps build a WORKING ALLIANCE between client and counsellor)—it has other benefits, particularly for staff working in institutional settings:

For clients
- contact work dissolves not only personal and social isolation, but also many of the secondary symptoms and coping behaviours associated with such isolation
- it enables communication of everyday needs, thus facilitating more efficient, targeted and personalised everyday care
- it facilitates emotional development
- it helps clients make informed treatment choices

For staff
- it generates more effectiveness and job satisfaction through a greater involvement in a healing relationship
- it creates a less threatening working environment since clients are less agitated when contact is established
- it develops deeper insight and understanding of the experience of out-of-contact clients

CLIENT PERCEPTION—AN IMPORTANT CONCEPT IMPLICIT IN CONTACT

A complementary idea to that of psychological contact is contained in Rogers' last condition where he writes:

> That the client perceives, at least to a minimal degree, conditions 4 and 5, the unconditional positive regard of the therapist for him, and the empathic understanding of the therapist. (Rogers, 1959: 213)

This final condition is confirming that the client has actually experienced the UPR and empathy that the counsellor has been offering. This is not a foregone conclusion and so Chapter 9 is devoted to an exploration of the whole idea. The client's perception of the counsellor's good intentions can no more be assumed than any other aspect of psychological contact.

It is possible, of course, that there *is* contact between the counsellor and client, but that even though the counsellor is *intending* to be understanding and non-judgemental, the client is not experiencing the counsellor as such.

This is why, in training, tutors and fellow students will give feedback about how the trainee counsellor is 'coming across'. Are they actually communicating empathy, UPR and so on, when they think they are? Only the client can answer that question, and indeed, each client is different, so where one client might think a particular counsellor *is* being empathic, another client may not.

If this sounds rather complicated at this stage, Chapter 9 explains further. The idea that the client's perception is important (actually 'necessary') drives home the foundation of person-centred practice—the client knows best. It is the client's perception of the relationship that is essential. This has to be our touchstone throughout person-centred work.

PRESENCE—A SPECIAL SORT OF CONTACT?

In 1986 Rogers described a phenomenon which he called 'presence' and 'one more characteristic' of the therapeutic relationship:

> when I am at my best ... closest to my inner, intuitive self, when I am somehow in touch with the unknown in me, when perhaps I am in a slightly altered state of consciousness in the relationship, then whatever I do seems full of healing. Then simply my presence is releasing and helpful. (Rogers, 1986, cited in Kirschenbaum & Henderson, 1990: 137)

This has been taken in different ways—some seeing it as evidence of a spiritual connection between counsellor and client, others as an additional quality or even therapeutic condition. It can also be taken to be a kind of momentary 'super-psychological contact'. Read the whole of the reference to make your own mind up.

5

THE CLIENT NEEDS HELP
(CLIENT INCONGRUENCE: CONDITION 2)

In 1957 and 1959 Rogers' second necessary condition for therapeutic change was:

> That the first person, whom we shall term the client, is in a state of incongruence, being vulnerable, or anxious. (Rogers, 1959: 213)

It might help if we unpack this statement a little. First, Rogers is making sure we understand that we are in a structured helping relationship (which may or may not be paid and 'professional'; as opposed to being unpaid and voluntary). He clearly identifies the role of the helped person as that of the client.

Second, he says that the client must be in a 'state of incongruence'. This, along with the phrase 'being vulnerable, or anxious' refers to Rogers' theory of personality and these are covered in more detail in Chapter 2 on personality and Chapter 3, the actualising tendency.

CLIENT INCONGRUENCE

The term 'congruence' crops up repeatedly in Rogers' work. Unfortunately, it means something slightly different in various contexts. In order to be absolutely clear, I am going to deliberately refer to it in different ways in different contexts, and so when talking about the client, I am going to use the term 'client incongruence'. Some other writings do not make this distinction, but in my view it is essential to avoid confusion.

Put very simply, Rogers is saying that *the client needs help, and knows it*. The client needs to have recognised that something is wrong, although they might not be able to say quite what it is that is wrong. Different helping theories describe this in different ways. Each set of terms gives something away about the type of approach the helper is using. Person-centred psychology is more interested in the *client's own description* of their distress.

Having a system of concepts and terms for describing and categorising distress is called PSYCHOPATHOLOGY (see Joseph & Worsley, 2005). It involves a *taxonomy* (system of classification) of the types of distress, and a method of *diagnosis* or system of identification of a condition. The most commonly used is the MEDICAL-MODEL classification of mental illness, but person-centred psychology does not fit with this system very well. Indeed many practitioners contend that it doesn't fit in at all and is, in fact, antagonistic to the MEDICAL MODEL. This has caused misunderstandings and negative perceptions of person-centred counselling over the years.

The other important aspect of this condition is connected to the client recognising that something is wrong, namely that the client has also voluntarily brought themselves along for counselling. They *want* to attend, or in psychological terms they are MOTIVATED to attend. This is an important element in a number of therapeutic approaches, but is particularly important in person-centred counselling since the theory tells us that the client is doing the changing themselves with the assistance of the counsellor. Obviously, this process of change from within needs the client to want it to happen. By definition, they *cannot* be changed in a person-centred way against their will.

Whilst this might seem obvious initially, it actually affects a wider range of helping situations than you might imagine, e.g.:

- Students in schools and colleges are sometimes asked to attend counselling as a condition of a punishment.
- Some clients are asked to attend counselling as a condition of staying in a relationship, e.g. one partner might threaten to end the relationship unless the other seeks help with their gambling/substance abuse/aggression, etc.
- Threats and inducements to change can also take place *inside* the person. There could be 'internal dialogue' where one part or 'CONFIGURATION' (Mearns, 1999) seeks change or counselling and another part does not.

THE CLIENT'S OWN EXPERIENCE

Person-centred theory has a number of features which positively point to the client's own experience as the best source of understanding their distress. These are covered in this book in various places but I want to draw attention to them point by point. Many people read this material and realise that this emphasis on the client's experience sets the person-centred approach against the dominant MEDICAL MODEL of mental illness used by many helping professionals. This is briefly debated at the end of the chapter.

Person-centred theory is PHENOMENOLOGICAL
PHENOMENOLOGY is a philosophical approach to understanding based on the experience and perceptions of the individual. So a PHENOMENOLOGICAL approach is based exclusively on the subjective experiences of the client. That is why *empathy* is so important in person-centred counselling. Not because it builds trust, but because the helping method is completely dependent on understanding the world of the client, rather than on understanding an external framework, like a theory of dream symbols, taxonomy of observable signs, or a diagnostic system.

Rogers stressed the importance of being non-directive
The significance of this should be obvious. If the counsellor is not intending to direct the content or process of the client's healing, they are, in effect, taking a non-expert stance. Such a stance cannot include any idea that the counsellor knows better than the client what it is that might be wrong with them.

Person-centred counselling tries to install an INTERNAL LOCUS OF CONTROL
The term 'INTERNAL LOCUS OF CONTROL' means that the person in question (the client in this case) is able to make emancipated autonomous decisions based on their own experience; literally controlling their lives from inside their world and feeling the sense of empowerment to achieve it. Person-centred counselling tries to help the client achieve independence.

This is very different from going to the doctor and submitting to his or her diagnosis and direction of treatment (an external LOCUS OF CONTROL: being directed from outside). In this way the

MEDICAL MODEL establishes dependence. Whilst this might be fine for physical illness, it is inappropriate, and can be positively damaging in the case of psychological and emotional distress.

Categorising and labelling people is the first step towards objectification

Carl Rogers objected to diagnosis and the MEDICAL MODEL on the basis that it pushed uniquely-shaped persons into regulation-shaped categories. *Signs* (objective evidence) and *symptoms* (subjective evidence) are used by MEDICAL-MODEL practitioners to help identify the supposed category of mental 'illness' in the MEDICAL MODEL. These categories (SCHIZOPHRENIA, clinical depression, etc.) are then used to assign treatments. Not only are these categories disputed and contentious even within the profession, person-centred therapists argue that the very act of categorisation is both damaging and dehumanising. It renders the whole therapeutic enterprise impossible because therapeutic change requires the most uncontaminated, detailed, subjective experience as its raw material (see PHENOMENOLOGY, above). Diagnosis destroys this.

The person-centred approach is wellness-oriented

This wouldn't be news until we realise that the MEDICAL MODEL is *illness*-oriented, and needs little amplification except to say that the person-centred approach is not alone in realising that how we see distress colours all of our actions. If we see distress as a 'deficit' or 'illness' or indicating that something is 'broken' requiring psycho-technological or PHARMACOLOGICAL intervention, we behave very differently than if we see distress as unrealised potential, requiring enhanced conditions for self-healing.

PERSON-CENTRED PSYCHOPATHOLOGY?

There are differing views on whether it is either possible or desirable that person-centred counselling could or should fit in with the MEDICAL MODEL. Students on diploma, degree or Masters courses will have to look in detail at this issue; further reading could include, Boy, 1989/2002; Wilkins, 2003: 99–107; and Joseph & Worsley, 2005. Certificate, or counselling skills students, on the other hand, may not have to make a professional decision, but as citizens and consumers of the healthcare system, it can be instructive to look briefly at the arguments for and against a person-centred PSYCHOPATHOLOGY or system of concepts and terms for describing and categorising distress.

Arguments against a person-centred PSYCHOPATHOLOGY
There are problems with the whole notion of PSYCHOPATHOLOGY and associated concepts from a person-centred point of view.[1] First, a person-centred way of thinking and working is not based on a deficit model.

Second, by and large,[2] person-centred theory proposes *one* cause of psychological distress or disturbance. This is not a simple *universal* theory, because although there is a single, universal cause for distress, it will manifest itself in a unique way in each individual. There will *never* be two cases the same. Similarly the practice of person-centred counselling suggests only *one* solution: the therapeutic conditions. But this universal solution is also never the same twice, since the therapeutic conditions are always manifested in a unique relationship between two unique persons. This combination of universal cause and solution manifesting in an infinite number of ways is more than a little difficult for the well-ordered world of the MEDICAL MODEL to cope with. It also explains why, if the client's experience is paramount, empathic understanding is such an important condition in the healing relationship, since empathic understanding is the quality which gains access to the client's experience.

Third, the entire field of psychology is rather uncomfortably based on medical science. I say *uncomfortably* because it actually

1. For a debate, see the symposium on psychodiagnosis (Boy, 1989/2002) and responses. For a recent critical position, see Sanders, 2005.
2. There are exceptions to and variations on this idea which could be called developments of person-centred theory. Of particular interest (although there are others) is the work of Mearns (1999: CONFIGURATIONS OF SELF); Mearns & Thorne (2000: social actualising tendency); and Warner (2000: fragile process).

makes no sense at all to base our understanding of human distress on a series of categories put together as though distress was an *illness*. I say '*as though* distress was an illness' because the MEDICAL MODEL for physical illness works on the basis of signs and symptoms leading to a unique diagnosis of a category; i.e. the *cause* of the signs and symptoms. Then the diagnosis points to a cure or solution to the signs and symptoms based on biological science. So, a patient with a certain specific type of abdominal pain (symptom) and fever (sign) is diagnosed with the category of illness called acute appendicitis (cause). The solution is to remove the appendix by surgery. Signs and symptoms lead to a physiologically related cause which points to a cure.

The phenomena of distress are not arranged like this since the symptoms and signs are only grouped according to similarity, not according to any biological science pointing to a causal category. Then the categories themselves are only arranged in order of similarity, because there is no biological framework within which to arrange them. This destroys any possible logic for the use of a 'cure' based on an assumed 'category'.

Taking a negative view of the MEDICAL MODEL and renouncing moves towards a person-centred PSYCHOPATHOLOGY does not mean that practitioners must inevitably turn their backs on working in settings where psychiatry and the MEDICAL MODEL provide the dominant ideology. Lisbeth Sommerbeck provides a model (Sommerbeck, 2003, 2005) based on the idea of complementarity or co-existence of models in which she describes in detail her way of working without compromising the therapist's non-authoritarian attitude. Sommerbeck acknowledges the tension between the approaches and works to protect the person-centred therapy process in the often antagonistic milieu of the psychiatric setting.

Arguments for a person-centred PSYCHOPATHOLOGY
Some writers argue for the development and installation of a person-centred PSYCHOPATHOLOGY, either as a part of, or alongside, the MEDICAL MODEL. There are various possible reasons for doing this, from thinking that the MEDICAL MODEL is a good classification and diagnostic system, and person-centred theory needs to adapt

to it, through to setting up a rival person-centred system of classification and diagnosis based on a new understanding of person-centred psychology. The extremes also represent a range of professional and political dynamics.[3]

Variations include applying person-centred theoretical explanations and treatment methods to existing categories (and establishing an evidential base) and this is favoured by some practitioners. Others believe that it is best to work within established frameworks such as the MEDICAL MODEL. In order to do this, they seek to develop new diagnostic categories more representative of person-centred psychology and install them in the MEDICAL-MODEL manuals. And still others see value in diagnosis and seek to establish credible alternatives to the whole model based on person-centred principles.

This whole range of possibilities is in evidence in the volume edited by Stephen Joseph and Richard Worsley (Joseph & Worsley, 2005) and readers drawn to an understanding of the person-centred approach in relation to existing MEDICAL-MODEL PSYCHOPATHOLOGY are directed to Elke Lambers' (2003) brief explorations and Paul Wilkins' overview of the issues (Wilkins, 2003).

Margaret Warner has done more than most to develop a person-centred PSYCHOPATHOLOGY and effect a reconciliation of the person-centred approach and the MEDICAL MODEL along the way. One of her simple and persuasive rationales argues that regardless of ideological differences, person-centred practitioners must develop theory which establishes the approach as a credible partner in the treatment of distressed people. Not to do so would be an abdication of responsibility to our clients *today*. We must acknowledge the reality that the medical system controls mental health treatment and, at least in the short term, develop theory and vocabulary—namely a person-centred PSYCHOPATHOLOGY— which helps us 'join the club' (Warner, 2005).

---

3. In case this seems to be getting too far removed from 'the client needing help', remember that every idea and practice in helping and counselling has a social and political context as well as a psychological framework. Nothing comes devoid of values and wider connections and it is best to try to understand these early on. Psychology must always relate to a context.

Warner's starting point is the notion of 'process'. In order to begin to understand this concept and its implications, readers will have to skip to Chapter 11. Suffice to say at this point that Warner is dedicated to developing a PSYCHOPATHOLOGY built upon person-centred theoretical foundations (rather than PSYCHODYNAMIC theory or quasi-medical PSYCHOPHARMACOLOGY), imbued with the person-centred sensibilities of health and actualisation (rather than illness and deficit which are the foundations of the MEDICAL MODEL), and which points towards person-centred practice (rather than COGNITIVE or PSYCHODYNAMIC practice, or PHARMACOLOGICAL management).

This last paragraph illustrates the size of Margaret Warner's task, since person-centred counselling is set against a medical way of thinking at almost every turn, from philosophy through theory to practice. In order to present a convincing alternative she must present a convincing option at each level. At this point, some readers can relax. It is enough to know at certificate level that person-centred counselling has at least one alternative to offer. Understanding those alternatives is reserved for diploma and Masters study.

Working out where you stand

At this stage, working out where you stand on the subject of PSYCHOPATHOLOGY is a tall order. It takes years of study and years of experience before people feel confident to adopt a position. Also, taking a position of 'I don't know' should not be seen as defeatist or woolly-mindedness. The truth is that whatever we might *want* to believe, experience can be a great educator. So anyone with experience of psychological distress or working in the field of mental health will have views based on their experience.

Another important point is that the facts are much more inconclusive than I have presented here. This chapter is intended to get you thinking, to start a debate. You might think my argument so far is weighted against the MEDICAL MODEL, and you would be right. I *am* against the MEDICAL MODEL for a number of personal and professional reasons, so I will not be able to disguise my bias. Finally, since the MEDICAL MODEL is around us everywhere in the 'helping professions' and presented *as though it is true*, I wanted to sow a few seeds of doubt to get the process of debate started.

6

THE COUNSELLOR IS READY TO HELP
(CONGRUENCE: CONDITION 3)

This is another condition which needs some introduction before we get down to the detailed description. What Rogers actually said was as follows:

> That the second person, whom we shall term the therapist, is congruent (*or integrated*) in the relationship. (Rogers, 1957 and 1959: 213, [words in italics appear in the 1957 paper but not in the 1959 chapter])

Again, we need to unpack this statement to get at Rogers' meaning. First, Rogers is reminding us that he is talking about a structured helping relationship in which the roles are clear.

Second, he is saying something about the basis on which the counsellor is offering help. In particular he is suggesting that, in this relationship at least, the counsellor has to be more congruent or integrated than the client. In simple terms he means that whilst the client *in this moment* may be feeling distressed and in need of help, the counsellor *in this moment* is not and is prepared to help.

In a structured helping relationship, the counsellor needs to be prepared to be the counsellor, and there are several ways of understanding 'be prepared to be'. This condition refers, at least in part, to the counsellor's fitness to help. In the same way that a driver must ensure that they are fit to drive every time they set out in a car, which includes:

- that they know how to drive and have passed their test
- they have not had too much (or any) alcohol, prescribed medicines or other substances which might impair their driving
- they feel psychologically able to drive, e.g. they are not driving off in a furious temper after an argument with their partner

In person-centred counselling this means that (see Chapter 2, pp. 19–20) the counsellor is congruent, able to be authentic, and open to their experience. Or at any rate, if they are to be of help, they must be congruent in relation to the client in that moment, i.e. given that everyone is incongruent to some degree, the counsellor is the one *in this relationship* that is more congruent.

A WORD OF CAUTION ON CONGRUENCE

It is true to say that congruence is one of the more controversial of Rogers' conditions. I have already mentioned that Rogers uses the word 'congruence' to mean different things in different settings (page 43). The idea of congruence meaning something to do with the preparedness of the counsellor to help is specific to condition 3. Look out for other meanings as you read through the book.

Readers should also remember that these conditions were written almost fifty years ago when psychiatry, psychology, counselling and helping in general were very different from today. In those days, psychological helping was largely educative, in other words the psychologist made suggestions or taught the patient different and new ways to think about and tackle problems. It was a fairly formal interview with the psychologist as the acknowledged expert, and referred to as 'Doctor ...' where appropriate. Congruence was something of a revolutionary concept in such a setting, as you can imagine. It might seem that today, in a relaxed informal helping relationship, the idea that the helper should 'be themselves' without a professional façade is practically a foregone conclusion. Remember that Rogers was writing to change the (in comparison to today) somewhat stuffy, advice-orientated helping behaviour in the 1950s.

CONGRUENCE 'IN THE RELATIONSHIP'

In Rogers' words, 'the therapist's SYMBOLISATION of his [*sic*] own experience in the relationship must be accurate' (1959: 214). This means that the counsellor should be open to their experience and be able to be themselves in the relationship without need for defence, façade, false front or professional guise. The requirement is that 'in this moment of this immediate relationship with this specific person, [the counsellor] is fully and completely himself [*sic*]' (ibid.: 214). In 1957, Rogers wrote similarly:

> [T]he therapist should be, within the confines of this relationship, a congruent, genuine integrated person. It means that within the relationship he is freely and deeply himself, with his actual experience accurately represented by his awareness of himself. (1957: 97)

Clearly, this quality is not something we would expect of the client. Colloquially we might say that we expect the counsellor to be more 'together' or more 'sorted' than the client. As a consequence we would expect the counsellor to be together enough to be comfortable and confident, and not to be defensive or self-conscious.

Expressing the difference between the counsellor and the client—between the client's need for help and the counsellor's readiness to offer help, is something that happens in all therapeutic approaches. In some approaches this difference is expressed as knowledge and expertise, i.e. that the counsellor *knows more* about psychology and therapy, and/or is *an expert* in teaching about how to change.

Person-centred counselling reveals how, *implicit in its theory*, it sets itself apart from expert-orientated approaches, since it is not exclusively *knowledge* and *expertise* that determine the differences in role between the counsellor and client. It is in their *state of preparedness as a person*. But not in some absolute sense, where we might be able to measure 'preparedness as a person' against some yardstick and then say with confidence, 'yes, this person can be a counsellor'. Rather it is measured in relation to the other person—the person in need of help.

Again, this points towards the unique *relationship* between the client and counsellor as holding all the clues, and as such it is difficult to make generalisations. Suffice to say that this means that the person-centred counsellor in one relationship can be the client in another. It also means that being a person-centred counsellor isn't a measure of how 'sorted out' you are in an absolute sense. It also means that being a person-centred counsellor doesn't mean having expert knowledge. It means being an expert in providing the right conditions for the actualising tendency *of the particular client you are with* to get on with the healing process.

THE MULTI-FACETED NATURE OF CONGRUENCE

This subtitle is borrowed from Gill Wyatt's (2000/2001) paper on congruence wherein she mapped out the various possible understandings of the concept of congruence in the family of person-centred therapies. She (Wyatt, 2001: 84–5) identified three core aspects of congruence: being myself, psychological maturity, and the personal style of the therapist. These aspects translate into facets of counsellor behaviour and they are all linked.

Being myself is fairly self-explanatory, meaning that the counsellor is authentic and 'real' rather than putting on a professional facade, or acting out the role of counsellor. I have put 'real' in inverted commas since some commentators (Frankel & Sommerbeck, 2005) claim that 'this issue of realness and genuineness is bogus' (p. 42) since a therapist, even in the role of therapist, is still 'really' in the role. This debate, though, is appropriate for diploma, degree and Masters-level students rather than this brief primer. My purpose is to alert readers to the differences of opinion in the person-centred community.

This facet of authentic 'true-to-the-person-I-truly-am' behaviour does resonate with a number of people. Many of us experience moments where we feel one thing and behave in a way that belies this. In everyday life we might do this for a number of reasons: to protect our own or someone else's feelings, to avoid conflict, or to achieve a desired result in a transaction. We decide to disguise our feelings to achieve a higher aim in the moment. The important issue is whether it is therapeutic to do this with a client. Whilst most people might say they prefer their counsellor to be 'honest' in the way they present themselves, this doesn't resolve the problem since even the term honesty has some elasticity in its meaning.

The concept of being myself is linked to both of the following facets of congruence.

Psychological maturity indicates the degree to which the

counsellor is open to their experience. This definition of congruence is the one Rogers uses in connection with his personality theory which I cover in Chapter 2. It is also linked to the notion of the split between the actualising tendency and self-actualisation I described in Chapter 3 starting at page 30. What is being described in both places is the relative harmony or disharmony in the personality structure of the counsellor. This incongruence in the personality leads to the potential for the counsellor to be vulnerable to experiences that they might not feel comfortable with.

It is the same factor we looked at briefly earlier in this chapter, where I said that colloquially we might say that the counsellor is 'sorted' or 'together'. One of the qualities of people who are 'sorted' is that they are open to their experience, they do not behave defensively, are open to looking at, or reflecting on, their own behaviour and their own personal qualities. In theoretical terms we might also say that this person is 'integrated': their personality is in harmony, or congruent.

This quality has important consequences in therapeutic situations. People who are more open to their experience and less defensive will have fewer areas of their make-up unavailable to them. They are more likely to feel comfortable about being their true self, as in the section above. In addition, the more open I am to my experience, the less threatened I will be by the challenging ideas and behaviour of other people. I will, therefore, be able to be more accepting of others. Finally, I will be able to use supervision and mentorship of my work better if I am open to reflecting on my behaviour and receiving feedback.

The personal style of the therapist refers not to *what* I do, but *how* I do it. It requires me to interpret the ground rules of being a person-centred counsellor in my own way, whilst, of course still staying within the 'rules'. In ballroom dancing, everyone has to learn the same steps in order to dance the foxtrot. Yet each dancer has their personal style which makes them a unique exponent of the dance, whilst still dancing a recognisable foxtrot.

It might be said that the most important factor is *how* something is said. For example, there are many ways a doctor can give a patient bad news. All might be technically 'honest', but there are brutal, tender, dismissive, understanding, flippant and over-concerned *ways* of being honest.

Readers should be aware that when talking about being 'honest' I am assuming that therapists are honest in the everyday content of discourse with their clients—this has never been in question. What I am talking about here is honesty in the way I present myself, i.e. not pretending or making myself out to be something I'm not. This can be something as simple as saying I'm relaxed, when in fact I am sad or tense (maybe as a result of the client's behaviour). I might say such a thing and be fully aware of the discrepancy, or I might be unaware that my discomfort is, in fact, sadness or tension that I am not admitting to awareness. This is a difficult dilemma when such a circumstance arises in a counselling session, and is the subject of continuing debate amongst person-centred practitioners. To be congruent means to be aware of the feeling of sadness if it arises in the counselling session, but not necessarily to do anything about it. The latter decision (to disclose my feeling of sadness) is one of therapeutic effectiveness and is a matter of judgement in each different case.

CONGRUENCE IN PRACTICE

Godfrey Barrett-Lennard outlined the qualities of 'the highly congruent individual' in 1962 as:

> completely honest, direct, and sincere in what he [*sic*] conveys, but he does not feel any compulsion to communicate his perceptions, or any need to withhold them for emotionally self-protective reasons. (1962: 4, cited in Barrett Lennard, 2002: 30)

This brings into sharp focus the requirements for practice. Staying with the example above, I can be honest, direct and sincere whilst having a feeling of sadness in a session with a client. If the feeling persists or I notice it happens when the client talks about missing his father, I might discuss the matter with my supervisor, since it might be that the feeling of sadness is my own feeling of missing *my* father. It would be inappropriate for me to disclose this to my client if this were the case. So congruence is the capacity to be open to experiences. In practice, the counsellor then decides what to do on the basis of experience or supervision.

Probably the most frequent debate regarding congruence on counselling and counselling skills training courses concerns the idea that therapist self-disclosure is congruent behaviour. Paul Wilkins is clear: 'Being congruent is *not* the same as self-disclosing' (2003: 82, original italics) and Sheila Haugh (2001: 116) cautions 'congruence does not mean "anything goes" (what I call the "I felt it so I said it" syndrome)'.

In 2002, Barrett-Lennard asks why 'a high level of therapist congruence is evidently beneficial …?' (p. 46) and he comes up with a number of reasons including:
- Congruence facilitates trust.
- It is the foundation of empathic and non-judgemental responses.
- It models openness and 'unguarded whole presence' so that the client might try out this otherwise risky behaviour.
- Therapist confidence in congruent behaviour might be infectious and encourage openness in the client.

The vocabulary of congruence—a summary
Sheila Haugh (Haugh, 2001) looked in detail at the problems generated by both the apparent different uses of the term congruence, and the apparent use of different terms to mean the same thing. Being real, genuineness, authenticity and transparency are all terms used at different times by person-centred writers to try to explain congruence. These terms have also been investigated and explained by Germain Lietaer (Lietaer, 1993/2001) and diploma-level students are directed to this work for a better understanding of the issues.

Haugh points out that the confusion arises because we are likely to use the common-use meanings of words such as genuineness, whereas Rogers used the term to mean exactly the same as his theoretical concept of congruence. The message, however, is clear—self-awareness in the counsellor is the key to congruence coupled in practice with clear, direct, sensitive communication.

7

UNCONDITIONAL POSITIVE REGARD
(CONDITION 4)

As we have seen, some of the therapeutic conditions had different wording in Rogers' 1957 and 1959 writings. Condition 4, however, was the same on both occasions:

> That the therapist is experiencing *unconditional positive regard* toward the client. (Rogers, 1959: 213, original emphasis)

Simple though the wording might appear, the concept of unconditional positive regard (UPR) has been hotly debated over the years. If you have not come across the term before, simply put it means that the counsellor listens in a non-judgementally warm way. Other words that have been used over the years to describe this condition are acceptance, respect and valuing (or prizing). There are two components to the concept, unconditionality and the positivity of regard, both of which have raised criticisms from various quarters in the psychotherapy community over the years. I will examine each of these components separately, but not before re-emphasising that the condition of UPR is useless unless the components are experienced as one indivisible attitude by the client. This also give me the opportunity to re-emphasise the core person-centred notion that *all* of the therapeutic conditions should be considered as one unified attitude towards clients, not separate elements or, worse still, skills.

WHY UPR?

Just like Rogers' other therapeutic conditions, there is traceable logic behind UPR, originally stemming this time from his theory of personality (Rogers, 1951: 481–533). This early work of Rogers can be a tough read for students without a background in psychology, but the same material is summarised (rather savagely, in order to fit the space) in Chapter 2 of this book.

Rogers organised his 'theory of personality and behaviour'

into nineteen propositions. Each statement builds on the previous ones to construct an almost complete theory of personality. I say 'almost complete' for two reasons: first, Rogers never considered his work to be complete, always a work in progress, and second, he updated it and filled in some missing pieces in his later work (Rogers, 1959).

We begin with the idea that, in early infancy, all human beings develop a need for positive regard, or *love*. Rogers stated that this need is 'universal ... pervasive and persistent' (1959: 223). In short, love is very satisfying and is an important survival component in infant relationships (we need to develop strong bonds with those around us on whom we have to depend to survive). The infant then develops a trust in its own experiences and this is called positive self-regard (the infant needs to develop this in order to become independent and make its own decisions). Of course, in most cases in the 'real world', the growing infant experiences a range of types and degrees of regard from others and themselves, both positive and negative.

Positive regard, however, remains very potent particularly, as I mentioned above, when it comes from people on whom we have to depend. Indeed it is so potent that in infancy, when someone close to us repeatedly threatens to withhold love if we don't think, feel and behave in particular ways, it sets up CONDITIONS OF WORTH, i.e. the conditions which determine our sense of worth in the world, e.g. 'you will only be lovable if you put the dolls away and play with boy's toys'. Over time, the child imports these repeated commands and the values attached to them into their developing personality. Worse still, although these judgements and values come from another person (however well-meaning) they are taken in to the SELF-STRUCTURE as though they were the child's own self-perceptions. This process is known as INTROJECTION.

Introjection is a problem because it sets up incongruence (disharmony) inside the SELF-STRUCTURE of the person. Whilst the child has its own intrinsic ORGANISMIC VALUING PROCESS, this gets outranked by INTROJECTED values since they appear, to the child, to be tied to survival. There is incongruence and tension in the SELF-STRUCTURE if the child gets pleasure from playing with dolls

(ORGANISMIC VALUING) but thinks it ought not to because it won't be loveable (INTROJECTED VALUES).

Simply put, the important active elements of the process of INTROJECTION are *conditionality* and *love* or *positive regard.* And so, the equally 'simple' method for undoing the potential or actual psychological distress that can result from the incongruence between ORGANISMIC VALUING and INTROJECTED valuing is to make the love or positive regard *unconditional.* This is the short answer to the question 'Why UPR?' A slightly longer answer involves a quick look at Proposition 17 from Rogers (1951: 517) writing mentioned earlier. Here he says: 'Under certain conditions, involving primarily complete absence of any threat to the self-structure ...' the SELF-STRUCTURE can be revised. One of the best ways of removing threat is to be non-judgemental, or in person-centred terms, be unconditional in your positive regard towards the client. Jerold Bozarth puts it most clearly and succinctly: 'unconditional positive regard is the curative factor in client-centred theory' (Bozarth, 1998: 83).

This also links to the idea that the infant has both a way of evaluating its experience from the 'inside' and another from the 'outside'. These are the two loci of evaluation, the *internal* LOCUS OF EVALUATION (my own experiences regarding what I like and don't like) and the *external* (other people's ideas of what is good and bad). As they grow up, an independent person would tend to use their own self-evaluations (internal locus) when they make decisions. However, as we have seen, when a person's SELF-STRUCTURE contains many INTROJECTS, this picture is clouded. Even the internal LOCUS OF EVALUATION is likely to be driven not by the ORGANISMIC VALUING PROCESS, but by the INTROJECTED VALUES which, although now residing inside the SELF-STRUCTURE, actually originated outside.

Again, the warm, non-judgemental attitude of the therapist provides the best condition in which the client can consider change.

POSITIVE REGARD

The positive regard element of this condition is not the same as 'liking' or 'being nice to' the client. Dave Mearns addresses this point 'these two concepts [liking and unconditional positive regard] do not have much in common' (Mearns, 2003: 3). Nor does it have anything to do with having similar values or beliefs to the client. These are all relatively superficial attitudes in comparison with the attitude of positive regard.

My preferred word to describe positive regard is 'prizing'; one that was used frequently by Rogers, although warmth and respect are also very good. These terms all convey something about the depth or genuineness of the attitude, i.e. that, as Tony Merry explained, 'can't be turned on and off like a tap' (Merry, 2002: 80). It's virtually impossible to affect a display of warmth towards someone, to 'put it on' without appearing false, phony and quite frankly, unpleasant.

Another question frequently asked (which also misses the point) is how can you *guarantee* to feel warm towards all of your clients? This question is helpful though, because it alludes to the condition of congruence and starts us on the right path for understanding the true nature of therapeutic warmth, prizing and respect. What we are aiming for is an attitude of positive prizing and respect.

One cliché that has some value here is 'love the sinner, not the sin'. This permits, or to some readers, *instructs* us to prize the person as a human being worthy of our warm attention as a counsellor (since that is the job we have chosen), without having to condone their behaviour.

On a different tack, as we explore person-centred theory and practice we will find that self-awareness in the therapist is centrally implicated. The more self-aware the counsellor is, the more they will know their own prejudices, based as they are on fear. The fewer prejudices the counsellor has, the less judgemental they will be.

UNCONDITIONALITY

Rogers' work has had many critics over the years, but few areas of theory have attracted more criticism than the idea of the *unconditionality* of positive regard. To paraphrase Rogers (1959:

208), the experience of receiving UPR is to feel that my counsellor doesn't value any of my disclosures about my experience more positively or negatively than any other. I don't feel that my experiences are judged. I feel accepted, 'warts and all'; my whole person is prized. Rogers writes:

> It is the fact that he feels and shows unconditional positive regard toward the experiences of which the client is frightened or ashamed, as well as toward the experiences with which the client is pleased or satisfied, that seems effective in bringing about change. (Rogers, 1959: 208)

We can see that the 'unconditionality' refers to the way the counsellor doesn't sort experiences into 'good', 'bad', 'better' or 'not so good' categories. So it follows that the counsellor is not going to prefer the client to talk about certain things or to talk in certain ways. The therapist creates, through unconditionality, a level playing field for all of the client's experiences to enjoy a fair game, so to speak.

Dave Mearns, when explaining his concept of 'CONFIGURATIONS OF SELF' (Mearns, 1999; Mearns & Thorne, 2000), notes that a client might have different internal selves or CONFIGURATIONS, each with its own distinct characteristics. Not multiple personalities, but more distinct than simply 'facets' of the same person. A client might say they have a 'depressed loser', 'controlling careerist' and 'optimist' CONFIGURATIONS. As mentioned above, the counsellor must create a level playing field for all of the client's CONFIGURATIONS, but it is easy to see how a counsellor, even without intending to, could tilt the playing field and favour one CONFIGURATION over the other two. This might be good practice in COGNITIVE therapy, where the configuration with the rational resolution to a difficulty might be favoured. However in person-centred therapy the counsellor is creating the conditions in which the client's actualising tendency can resolve the tension and move forward regardless of which CONFIGURATION might hold the key. For this to take place, 'dialogue' between all CONFIGURATIONS is desirable and may even be necessary and so each must be equally valued.

Creating a level playing field might sound easy for an idealised counsellor, a theoretically perfect practitioner, but in practice some situations might arise which need exploration. When a person-centred counsellor has difficulty with a client because they feel conditional in their regard, or judgemental towards them (we are only human, after all), we have a couple of options.

Counsellors would be ill-advised to work in an area where they know themselves to be vulnerable or which conflicts with their values. Jeffrey Masson (1992: 234), for example, asks: 'Faced with a brutal rapist who murders children, why should any therapist have unconditional regard for him?' This point is covered above since it is possible to prize the person without condoning their behaviour. There are counsellors who can work with such clients without feeling judgemental, although I might not be one of them. Having worked hard to increase my self-awareness, I am therefore behoven to *not* work in a clinic that specialises in working with perpetrators of child abuse and murderers, if after my self-exploration I am unable to be with such people with an open, accepting attitude.

Life can still test us, however hard we try to account for our strengths and weaknesses, and when face to face with a client we have difficulty in prizing, we must be either sensitive and honest about our difficulty (saying it's *our* problem, not blaming them), or keep going in the session and take the issue to supervision as soon as possible.

Others question the whole notion of unconditionality, claiming that it is plainly impossible to *guarantee* it. Paul Wilkins makes the very good point that just because people find the theory difficult to put into practice, doesn't make it invalid:

> Theory asserts that if (for example) a paedophile consistently experiences the six conditions, then therapeutic change *will* occur. Of course it may be that this is a big 'if'. But what is important is that it is realised that the limitation is in the practitioner, not the theory. (Wilkins, 2003: 73, original emphasis)

My own answer to this criticism is that psychotherapy in general and person-centred therapy in particular is therapy by humans, with humans, for humans. Therein lies its strengths and weaknesses and the celebrated human characteristics of uncertainty and fallibility, and therefore the possibility of disappointment. Therapy with a robot would, naturally, remove these nuisances to perfect practice. I make this point with only a trace of a smile. It really is the reality of the human contact with all of its potential flaws, and all of its wonderful potential moments of validation and joy that makes therapy work (see also the work of Art Bohart briefly covered on pages 79 and 91–2). And having said that, it is also true that clients do better with therapists who are consistent—there is safety in routine.

One more, possibly paradoxical, point is to realise that most clients are not 'defined by their problem'—they like to be seen as multi-dimensional, rounded (if distressed) human beings. Even many victims of crime or abuse do not see themselves as entirely defined by such events or, worse still 'labels'. This is why UPR is such a valuable initial attitude for all counsellors and why person-centred counsellors make every effort to maintain it. So another message here is, beware of an explanation which leaves out the client's and the counsellor's unique processes—relationships are interactions on many dimensions.

Finally, I have found in my own practice that my most useful ally in UPR is empathy. Once I enter into the client's world a number of things happen: I encounter them as a person not a stereotype or 'demon'; I am more likely to understand the reasons behind their behaviour; and I am more likely to think 'there but by good fortune, go I'. I then find it difficult if not impossible to be judgemental.

8

EMPATHY
(CONDITION 5)

Rogers wrote the following in 1957 and 1959 regarding the fifth of his therapeutic conditions (the text in italics appeared in the 1957 paper only):

> That the therapist is experiencing an empathic understanding of the client's INTERNAL FRAME OF REFERENCE *(and endeavours to communicate this to the client).* (Rogers, 1959: 213)

This condition is presented in a fairly straightforward manner. Although some academics dissect the meaning of the term 'empathic understanding' as opposed to 'empathy', and the meaning of the extra words (in italics above), I do not think that the debates add much to a basic understanding of person-centred counselling. A unilateral experiencing of empathy, for example, is almost certainly impossible, since implicit in the experience of empathy is the idea of checking that you are accurate. Otherwise we would use the terms 'imagination' or 'guessing' to name the activity. So, implicit in the experiencing of empathic understanding is the experience of checking that your understanding is accurate. Communication is, therefore, an essential ingredient.

The term INTERNAL FRAME OF REFERENCE is a psychological term which means, in everyday language, a person's private world of perceptions, experiences and meanings. Only I can know my INTERNAL FRAME OF REFERENCE fully. According to Rogers, 'It can never be known to another except through empathic inference and then can never be perfectly known' (Rogers, 1959: 210).

Further clarification is also required regarding the texts that use the term 'accurate empathy' as though there could be such a thing as *inaccurate* empathy. Such an idea is not a part of person-centred theory—implicit in the concept of empathy is that it is an accurate understanding.

> … being empathic is to *perceive* the INTERNAL FRAME OF REFERENCE of another with *accuracy*, and with the emotional components and

> meanings ... *as if* one were the other person, but without ever
> losing the 'as if' condition. (Rogers, 1959: 210, my italics)

I have emphasised what I think are the key words in the quote. I want to stress that the empathic counsellor perceives the world of the other person, but does not experience it. I cannot *feel* someone else's hurt, fears and joys. I can, though, see their thoughts and feelings accurately and *understand* them.

The other essential component of this condition is communication: 'and endeavours to communicate this to the client' (Rogers, 1957, in Kirschenbaum & Henderson, 1990: 221). Empathy experienced by the therapist, without communicating it to the client, is of little or no use. So, nodding and saying 'Uh-huh', or 'Mm hmm' every few seconds for five minutes while the client tells their story *is not fulfilling condition 5 and therefore will not be therapeutic.* Rogers reinforces this point in condition 6 'the client perceives ... the empathic understanding of the therapist' (Rogers 1959: 213). Even occasionally interjecting 'I understand', or 'I see', is *not* an adequate communication of empathy. Viewing a few minutes of Carl Rogers or any other skilled therapist will confirm that empathy and its communication is a much more complex and *active* affair.

WHAT ROGERS SAID ABOUT EMPATHY

Rogers' last major statement about empathy 'Empathic: An Unappreciated Way of Being' was made in 1975 and reprinted in his book *A Way of Being* (Rogers, 1980). Here he writes about the *process* of empathy, rather than the *state* of empathy as 'being sensitive, moment by moment, to the changing felt meanings which flow in this other person' (p. 142) and that we have to 'lay aside your own views and values in order to enter another's world without prejudice' (p. 143).

I imagine this writing does not present much that is startlingly new to a twenty-first century reader. However, it is widely thought that Rogers was writing this in an effort to rehabilitate empathy, to restore it as the focal point of person-centred theory, since in many people's eyes, therapist congruence had become the most important 'core' condition. To give an idea of how the client might experience empathy, Rogers quoted an item from Goff Barrett-Lennard's Relationship Inventory (BLRI), thus: 'He understands what my experience feels like to me' (Barrett-Lennard, 1962, cited in Rogers, 1980: 143). This is the now-common understanding of the experience of empathy.

WHY IS EMPATHY IMPORTANT?

The 'classical' view

Although 'understanding' has always been implicit in practically all psychotherapy practice, regardless of theoretical orientation, the concept of empathy has a unique function in person-centred counselling. Our starting point (in terms of person-centred theory) to understanding why counsellors would find it useful to be empathic at all, is Rogers personality theory (Rogers, 1951).

It is important to understand that when Carl Rogers wrote his early books, he was trying to do at least three things simultaneously. First, he was trying to explain his new approach to therapy. Second, he was trying to make it credible in psychological circles at the time (which meant choosing his language carefully, following scientific conventions, etc.). Third, he was trying to show how his theory and practice was different from the established theories at the time, namely PSYCHOANALYSIS and BEHAVIOURISM. Nowadays this might seem like a historical footnote, but when we look closely we can see how, in 1951, he paved the way for empathy.

Rogers begins his writing on personality by establishing the PHENOMENOLOGICAL basis of his theory. He declares that the organism's perceptions are the basis for the organism's experience of reality. This might not seem so revolutionary nowadays, but hitherto, ordinary people were not expected to have a view about reality. For example, a couple of hundred years or so ago, to get a view on spiritual 'reality' one would go to a priest; for legal 'reality' a judge; and for health 'reality', a doctor. It is easy to see, then, how the idea of going to see a 'mind expert' would be the best way of getting a good picture of your state of mental health. The mind experts were the experts on your 'mental health reality', whether they were psychoanalysts interpreting your thoughts and dreams, or a behaviourist observing and attributing your behaviour.

Rogers put the understanding of reality in the eyes of the beholder of that reality. He then explained that the actualising tendency (see Chapter 3) motivated behaviour of the organism to 'satisfy its needs as experienced *in the field as perceived*' (Rogers, 1951: 491, my emphasis). So behaviour was driven by the actualising tendency according to the individual's own experience of reality. It was a private world of experience known only to the individual. This was very different from both PSYCHOANALYTICAL and BEHAVIOURIST ways of understanding behaviour. They relied on the experts understanding of reality (through their training and their theory) in order to know best what the client needed.

The best, indeed the *only*, way of relating to this private world of experience is through empathy. All the textbooks and theories in the world will not help you understand the client sitting in front of you.

Empathy as a principle or empathy as an instrument?
In Chapter 1 I mentioned the distinction between principled and instrumental non-directivity (Grant, 1990/2002). All of the active factors (whether you think of them as skills, conditions or attitudes) can be thought of as either a principle held in the counsellor's value-set, or as instruments employed for a particular purpose. Empathy is the therapeutic condition most amenable to being seen as a 'skill', but is no different in that it can be offered by the therapist in a principled way too.

The essential difference between the two is whether you are *using* empathy as a means to an end. Possible 'ends' might be to learn about the client's world so that you can build a trusting relationship with the client, diagnose a condition, or make helpful suggestions. Classical client-centred counselling (see Chapter 1, p. 14 and Merry, 2004) might also be referred to as non-directive client-centred counselling and is the strand of practice which is most likely to be *principled* in the holding of non-directivity and the other therapist-provided conditions as attitudes. Indeed, some classical non-directive client-centred practitioners cast person-centred therapy not as a psychological theory of change, but as an ethical stance. Most recently Peter Schmid (Schmid, 2001) shows how empathy fits into such an ethical scheme.

I realise that I am now inviting the reader into complicated territory. Too complicated for certificate or counselling skills-level learning, but if you intend to progress to professional training, diploma or degree, you must be prepared to engage with some serious thinking. The work of Grant (1990/2002, 2004, 2005) and Schmid (2001) are the starting points for such learning.

Other views—building on classical empathy

Rogers' early writing established why empathy is a good thing to do. Grant explained how empathy can be an ethical position without any therapist agenda concerned with 'information gathering', clarification or self-understanding. Others also asked what role it has in the change process but this level of theory is again a step or two above what might be expected at certificate level. I have summarised some of the ideas with appropriate references in case you want to chase them up:

- *Godfrey 'Goff' Barrett-Lennard* summarised the traditional idea that counsellor empathy facilitates self-empathy or 'listening within'. Self-understanding in a non-judgemental atmosphere begets self-acceptance which facilitates integration of previously difficult areas of experience (Barrett-Lennard, 2003: 34–50).
- *Eugene Gendlin* proposed that empathy moves the client's experience forward by allowing the client to monitor their experience through the repeated reflections and checking of the counsellor (see Purton, 2004).
- *Fred Zimring* proposed that empathy helps us shift our way of processing from an objective 'me' self-state to an inward-looking subjective 'I' self-state, making internal SELF-STRUCTURE change more possible (Zimring, 2000/2001).
- *Margaret Warner* in a similar vein to Gendlin, writes of how empathy fosters the ability to hold experiences in attention

in ways that stimulate personal growth (self-understanding depends on our ability to stay with or 'hold' an experience for long enough for us to engage with it). This is particularly important in infancy (and parenting) and has a crucial role in healthy personality development (Warner, 1997).

EMPATHY—MORE THAN JUST 'UNDERSTANDING'

Empathy is arguably the most written about therapist quality across all therapeutic orientations, and even if it *were* simply 'understanding', no therapy theory suggests that it is a bad thing to be doing. Empathy has received a lot of attention from client/ person-centred theorists and practitioners over the last thirty years and it will help to know some of the developments which have become woven into contemporary understandings of person-centred counselling. Discovering where you stand with regard to empathy will help you determine what type of person-centred counsellor you are, or want to be—which of the 'tribes' (Sanders, 2004) you most closely identify with.

Empathy as 'following' or empathy as 'evocative'

When you first start training in counselling or counselling skills, you no doubt get plenty of practice 'reflecting'. That is, more-or-less saying back to the client what they have said to you. You might paraphrase a long client statement and check that you have paraphrased correctly. Such responses are the basis of empathy as 'following the client'. Although wooden and awkward when you first try it, John Shlien declared:

> 'Reflection' is unfairly damned ... It is an instrument of artistic virtuosity in the hands of a sincere, intelligent, empathic listener.
> (Shlien, 1986, cited in Rogers, 1986/2002: 13)

Barbara Brodley has been foremost in developing reflection into what is now know as 'empathic following responses'—a self-explanatory term meaning tentative, open-to-correction reflective responses which follow the client. The counsellor never interprets, guesses or goes beyond what the client has said or indicated. The responses form the basis of what Brodley call the *empathic understanding response process*—a client-led exploration of experience, followed by the counsellor who checks the accuracy of their (the counsellor's) understanding at every turn. The best account of the surprisingly wide range of responses possible in this process is given in Brodley (2002).

In 1974, Laura North Rice gave voice to a growing tendency to be empathic in a way which went beyond the immediate expressions of the client. Such responses were said to attend to the implicit in the client's communications and extrapolate from the actual utterances of the client to open up potential experiences rather than simply to follow. Rice (1974/2001) described this as 'unfolding' the client's experience and called it *evocative empathy.* The aim is both to 'bring to life what it is like to be the client in that situation' (Rice, 1974/2001: 121) and enable the client to progressively deepen and enrich their experience through ever more accurate constructions and expressions of that experience.

Although these two 'modes' of empathy might appear very different (at least in their intentions), I have some difficulty in distinguishing between the two from the examples given in, for example, the references given above. You might encounter this phenomenon yourself when reading very vigorous debates between therapists or whole approaches claiming to be as different as chalk and cheese on paper. Although it is not *always* the case, frequently when you take a close look at exactly what they *do*, the differences begin to diminish and sometimes disappear.

Idiosyncratic empathy

When Jerold Bozarth (1984/2001: 138) stated unequivocally that 'reflection is not empathy', he meant that empathy is the *state* of *effort-to-accurately-understand* that the therapist is trying to communicate to the client. Reflection is just one of the responses, according to Bozarth, through which empathy may be communicated and he goes on to make a case for a much wider set of responses than Brodley (2002). His main point is to emphasise the idiosyncratic nature of human communication and suggests that using metaphor, personal reactions, mimicry and even jokes indicate that the therapist is empathic. We have to be careful that this doesn't become an excuse for the counsellor to do practically anything in the name of idiosyncratic empathy. Where would you draw the line?

Reverberative empathy

In a vibrant collection updating empathy in the late 90s (Bohart & Greenberg, 1997), John Shlien (1997/2001/2003) revisited a case first presented in 1961 (Shlien 1961/2003). He cites empathy as an essential and fairly basic human faculty which involves all senses. The case involves Mike (a former navy frogman incarcerated in a long-stay hospital with a diagnosis of SCHIZOPHRENIA), tears, the offer (and withdrawal) of a snotty handkerchief, and glances. There is a little more on this on page 75 of this book, but for a full account of this moving exchange see Shlien (1961/2003). Shlien describes empathy which 'reverberates', sometimes wordlessly, at a speed beyond the ability of speech: 'a series of "bouncing between us" consequences for each and for both' (Shlien, 1997/2003: 50). The healing property of such empathy consists in the affirming experience of knowing another and being known by another. Shlien argues that the whole construct of a 'self' is based on the existence of other selves. What would the point be of only one 'self' in the world? In order for one self to have any purpose or meaning there must be another self for it to relate to. Shlien states that human psychological health resides in selves knowing and being known, therefore empathy is the foundational human faculty for this health. Earlier he had written (Shlien 1984/2003: 110): 'misunderstanding is a form of hate-making' to indicate the absolutely affirming, healing and life-giving properties of being understood.

Empathy as the art of not-knowing

This subhead is taken from the title of a chapter by Peter Schmid (2001) 'Comprehension: The art of not-knowing …' It gives the reader clear clues to the DIALOGICAL view of empathy, namely that empathy as a human attribute comes without a particular intention but always as an expression of the personal quality of solidarity'

(p. 53). Schmid's work tackles the fundamentals of why and how human beings have relationships.

This work isn't easy to summarise, but for now, suffice to say he explains that human beings only exist in relation to each other (not a dissimilar position to Shlien's, above) and that empathy is a natural and essential part of being human. However, we are not empathic to achieve a particular end, such as learning about the world or people in it. We are empathic in a principled non-directive way because we *must be* in order to be human and relate to others. So empathy in a therapy relationship is an expression of flourishing human being, and restores this quality in others.

Other contributions

I must apologise to the theorists mentioned in this section, I don't intend it to be a collection of 'also-rans', but space limitations mean that only very abbreviated summaries are possible.

Mick Cooper reasoned that empathy is an embodied (i.e. expressed as a *physical, bodily* sense or symptom) experience since it requires the therapist to understand the *feelings* of the client. He explores all of the ways that the therapist resonates with the client's physical presence and draws attention to this domain of relating (Cooper, 2001).

Rose Cameron extends understanding of empathy beyond the COGNITIVE, affective and even physical to the domain of 'subtle' or psychic energy (some people might think of this energy in spiritual or transpersonal terms) as she writes of 'sensing' the client through energetic contact (Cameron, 2002).

Richard Baughan and *Tony Merry* reinforce the idea of empathy as essential humanity, but from an evolutionary/biological viewpoint. They see the roots of empathy, present at birth in humans, as an ADAPTATION whereby to know our own mental states and the mental states of others is a definite benefit to survival (Baughan & Merry, 2001).

Continuing developments in the elaboration of empathy include the importance of engaging with and understanding the person *in context* (i.e. their social and cultural context). See Proctor & Napier (2004), Moodley et al. (2004) and Proctor et al. (2006).

9

THE CLIENT FEELS UNDERSTOOD AND ACCEPTED
(CLIENT PERCEPTION: CONDITION 6)

The final condition is rarely quoted and even more rarely written about, yet it is absolutely paramount to successful therapy. So ignored was it that Keith Tudor was moved to refer to it as one of the 'lost' conditions (Tudor, 2000). Recently the situation has been rectified somewhat by Wyatt and Sanders (2002).

> The client perceives, at least to a minimal degree, conditions 4 and 5, the unconditional regard of the therapist for him, and the empathic understanding of the therapist. (Rogers, 1959: 213)

In simple terms, then, the client must have the empathy and UPR that the therapist is feeling communicated to him or her. They must experience the therapist as understanding and accepting. This reveals the all important final step in the client–counsellor relationship: communication of the therapist attitudes. Just thinking you are empathic or feeling accepting isn't enough. The counsellor must communicate this to the client *and the client must receive it*.

Condition 6 is further evidence that Rogers put the client at the centre of the process by insisting that therapy could not be effective unless the client—the key person in the relationship— experienced the counsellor as non-judgemental and empathic.

In counsellor training, this essential element is tackled in a couple of ways which rely on the natural characteristics of human communication. One way is through group experiences, personal development groups for example. The other is by being given feedback on your counselling by tutors or fellow students.

COMMUNICATION

The essence of any relationship is communication and human communication requires some sort of feedback loop, mutual recognition, a turn-taking where there is a to-ing and fro-ing of information sometimes referred to as 'interlocution'. It doesn't have to be verbal, and Rogers even suggested that it could be on the edge of awareness, only dimly recognised, but it must be there, detectable to the client.

Now starts an interesting discussion regarding how these sometimes subtle, sometimes in-your-face and sometimes marginal moments of communication are best understood. The first point to be made is that counsellor expressions will have to be varied—communication *cannot* be limited to head nodding and saying 'I see' or 'um hmm'. Whilst those communications may help the client feel in contact with the counsellor they do not give huge amounts of detail about understanding and acceptance.

The truly complex multiple layers of communication are illustrated well by John Shlien in this account of a fleeting moment in a session with 'Mike' an ex-navy frogman, diagnosed with 'paranoid SCHIZOPHRENIA' and incarcerated in a mental hospital. It is the late 1950s:

> [He] began to cry softly saying, 'they talk about needing love and affection. I know what *that* means. The only good thing I ever had (his engagement to a girl) taken away from me, broken up.' He blew his nose, dropped his handkerchief, and as he picked it up, glanced at me. He saw tears in my eyes. He offered me the handkerchief, then drew it back because he knew he had just wiped his nose on it and could feel the wetness on his hand. We both knew this, each knew the other knew it; we both understood the feel and the meaning of the handkerchief (the stickiness and texture, the sympathy of the offering and the embarrassment of the withdrawal) and we acknowledged each other and the interplay of each one's significance to the other. It is not the tears, but the exquisite awareness of dual experience that restores consciousness of self. (Shlien, 1961/2003: 57–8)

The moment of 'exquisite awareness' is only remarkable because of the way John Shlien captured it for us. They actually happen everyday between people if only we take the trouble to see them. In counselling we must pay attention all the time, not only to our client and their world, but to the way we relate to the person in front of us.

Whilst training it is important to realise that being a good communicator of these core therapeutic attitudes may well be difficult to begin with. If these qualities did not need development there would be no need for training. The best person to give you feedback on the qualities of your communication as a beginning counsellor is your client. A further important question, then, is 'How do I know that my client has perceived me as empathic and non-judgemental?' Beginning in the late 1950s Goff Barrett-Lennard tried to answer just this question.

CLIENT PERCEPTION

Carl Rogers made it clear that the client was the centre of the therapeutic process and furthermore it was the client who had the final say as to whether the 'therapist-provided conditions' were actually *provided* (as opposed to being assumed by the therapist). The fact is, however, that very few counsellors actually check to see how the client experiences them. Whilst we might have our ideas as to why counsellors might be reluctant to ask clients, it was an important research issue in the late 1950s, and Goff Barrett-Lennard set about exploring it in detail in his 1959 doctoral thesis. Three years later he had refined his work into a questionnaire-style psychological test which could be given to clients at various points in the counselling relationship, (Barrett-Lennard, 1962).

The Barrett-Lennard Relationship Inventory (BLRI) crystallises the therapist-provided conditions into statements (64 in the commonly-used version). The client is then asked to rate their counsellor in relation to them on a scale from +3 (strongly feel it's true) to –3 (strongly feel it's untrue), e.g.:

17. _____ is indifferent to me.

30. _____ realises what I mean even when I have difficulty in saying it.

52. There are times when I feel that _____'s outward response to me is quite different from the way he/she feels underneath. (Barrett-Lennard, 2002: 31)

Although the BLRI was used in a few research studies in the early 1960s, it never really caught on (tests purporting to measure the *outcome* of counselling have been much more popular) and is not a frequently used measure today, even in person-centred circles. It remains, however, a valid and RELIABLE test of the quality of the therapeutic relationship and Barrett-Lennard's work did, for a brief moment, raise the profile of client perception. As helpers and counsellors proceed in their training (to whatever level), they would do well to occasionally ask themselves 'How is my client receiving me? What is the *quality* of my relationship with this client?' The BLRI can be very useful if we want a valid answer. For more background on the BLRI and Barrett-Lennard's work on client perception, see Barrett-Lennard (2002, 2003: 93–112).

Another contribution to our understanding of client perception was made by another of Rogers' early co-workers (using the BLRI and other measuring instruments), Ferdinand Van der Veen, in 1970. Van der Veen presented data collected in conjunction with the WISCONSIN PROJECT, 1961, in which he discovered:

1. clients thought that therapists provided more of the therapeutic conditions than non-therapists;
2. clients who were more psychologically adjusted and had higher levels of process (see Chapter 11) thought that the therapists provided better therapeutic conditions;
3. clients improved more when they thought the therapists provided better conditions;
4. clients improved more when independent observers thought the therapists provided better conditions.

This research supplies the evidence that counselling is generally more effective when the client experiences the counsellor as providing good therapeutic conditions of understanding, authenticity and acceptance. However, we must not jump to conclusions—there could be more than one reason why the client is unable to experience the counsellor as warm, non-judgemental, real and empathic. Van der Veen suggests that differences in age, background or social class of the client might be stumbling blocks to good communication (Van der Veen, 1970) and nowadays we might add socio-cultural differences.

THE OTHER SIDE OF THE COIN

Having arrived at condition number 6, we might consider client perception, dependent on good communication, as the flip side of psychological contact. You can't have contact without perception, nor perception without contact. Whilst this is true of the other conditions as well, both client perception and psychological contact are to a great degree dependent on the effort put in by the counsellor to make a relationship connection with the client. And by the same token, dependent on the effort put in by the client to enter into a relationship with the potential for change.

The reason I mention this is that it relates particularly to the idea of the 'process of change' (the subject of Chapter 11), which in turn is dependent upon the degree to which the client is able to be in touch with their own experience. Don't worry if this appears to be going around in circles, since in a way it is. Fearful, vulnerable people protect themselves by closing down and shutting out threatening experiences. Person-centred counselling is a way of relating that is the least threatening—and Rogers explicitly acknowledges this in Proposition 17 (Rogers, 1951: 517): 'Under certain conditions, involving primarily complete absence of any threat to the SELF-STRUCTURE ...'. As people experience these non-threatening conditions, they begin to loosen this tight, protective way of organising their defences and they then see more of the therapeutic conditions that the counsellor is offering. So a non-threatening relationship—the six therapeutic conditions we have now covered—becomes a virtuous cycle. However, one ingredient, not formally acknowledged in the six conditions but implicit in them, runs through the relationship, namely *non-directivity*. The next chapter is devoted to this controversial concept.

THE CLIENT AS 'ACTIVE SELF-HEALER'

This phrase comes from Art Bohart who asked the sensible question 'How do clients make therapy work?' (Bohart, 2004; Bohart & Tallman, 1999). The phrase is also a central tenet of person-centred therapy, since we understand that it is clients who make therapy work, and counsellors who provide the conditions for them to achieve this. Bohart has put together a theory to explain just how clients use therapist responses, providing evidence that client's even make positive use of therapists' poor ('vapid, stereotyped and superficial', Bohart, 2004: 109) responses. Readers aiming for diploma-level study will find Bohart's work fascinating and I will look at a little more of this work on page 91–2.

10

BEING NON-DIRECTIVE

INTRODUCTION

Readers may have noticed that many chapters have started off
with me suggesting that the condition in question was in some
way controversial. I'm afraid that controversy will continue to
feature in this book even though we have now left the therapeutic
conditions behind on our journey. Non-directivity as a concept
still has the power to ignite passionate disagreement. For some it
is the keystone, the *raison-d'être* of practice in psychotherapy;
for others it is an ill-defined, or frankly impossible nonsense.

WHAT ROGERS WROTE ABOUT NON-DIRECTIVITY

The fifth chapter of Carl Rogers' 1942 book, *Counseling and
Psychotherapy*, was titled 'The directive versus the non-directive
approach'. His work at this time was influenced by Otto Rank
and Jesse Taft, and according to Raskin (1948/2004: 19) Rogers
gave 'the Rankian "client-as-central-figure" philosophy a definite
technique'. Readers should be aware that at this early stage in the
development of Rogers' ideas, the typical therapist believed
themselves to be an expert in understanding the client's behaviour
and asked many direct questions in order to come to a diagnosis.
They explained the client's problem to them and gave them lots
of information and advice on how to overcome it, including
homework. The therapist would point out faulty areas that needed
correction and try to persuade the client to take his or her advice.
Rogers' 'non-directive approach' pretty much turned this method
on its head. Quotes from his 1942 book set the scene:

> [Behind] differences between the directive and non-directive
> approaches lie deeper differences in the philosophy of counseling.
> … Non-directive counseling is based on the assumption that
> the client has the right to select his own life goals, even though

these might be at variance with the goals that the counselor might choose for him.

... There is also the belief that if the individual has a modicum of insight into himself and his problems, he will be likely to make his choice wisely.

... The non-directive approach places a high value on the right of every individual to be psychologically independent and to maintain his psychological integrity. (pp. 126–7)

In the intervening years, many things have changed in societal attitudes in general and the helping professions. Nowadays readers may well think that the quotes are mainstream assumptions in the helping professions of the twenty-first century. Rogers appears to have stayed true to his early understanding of the importance of non-directivity in his later years:

I still feel that the person who should guide the client's life is the client. My whole philosophy and whole approach is to strengthen him in that way of being, that he's in charge of his own life and nothing I say is intended to take that capacity or opportunity away from him. (Rogers, in Evans, 1975: 26)

It is clear then, that to practice in a way that stays true to Rogers' own understanding of person-centred counselling is to put the client at the centre and to not do anything that disempowers or disenfranchises the client. The question is, how does the counsellor behave in order to ensure that these values are both implicit and explicit in the helping the client receives?

CONTEMPORARY THINKING ON NON-DIRECTIVITY

Classical client-centred counsellors are more likely to rate non-directivity as an important central concept in their work, and a few have made important contributions to our appreciation of non-directivity in the past 30 years. Firstly, Nat Raskin originally outlined the concept in the 1940s (Raskin, 1948/2004, 2005), and Barbara Brodley has done much to maintain and develop the approach in the face of changing fashions in psychotherapy (e.g.

Brodley, 1999/2005). Barry Grant, mentioned in several places in this book, contributed the most original work on the essential differences between 'principled' and 'instrumental' non-directivity. With others he has developed the concept of an 'ethics-only' approach to counselling (Grant, 1990/2002, 2004, 2005) wherein the counsellor has *no goals or clinical objectives*—the counsellor operates *entirely* from an philosohical/ethical stance. Students taking their studies in person-centred therapy to diploma level or higher should regard Grant's writings as essential.

In summary (for a little more detail on Grant's work see below), non-directivity is seen as:

- Whilst not *formalised* in Rogers' theory (Rogers, 1957, 1959), it is none-the-less *implicit* in Rogers' work.
- An *attitude* not a set of behaviours or as technique. In experienced therapists it is an aspect of character.
- Finding expression through the therapeutic conditions and is inseparable from them—all therapist responses should be 'tempered' by non-directivity (Brodley, 1999/2005).
- According to Brodley (1999/2005: 3) 'Rogers … remained committed to the non-directive attitude. It is in the bones of his theory and practice.'

To illuminate the notion of the non-directive *attitude*, Barbara Brodley (1999/2005: 1) points out that attitudes are defined in terms of 'intentions, sensibilities, feelings and values', and that, with the exception of values, these qualities are likely to change slightly according to different circumstances, and so cannot be seen in theory as rigid rules or in practice as unchanging, repetitive responses.

Even the contemporary contributors would say that the core of the concept has changed little in the 60 or so years since Rogers outlined it, namely, a disciplined internalised intention to do everything possible to allow the client to determine the content, direction and to a large extent, the process of the therapy. When I say 'to a large extent' I mean that there are limits to what a client might reasonably expect the counsellor to do. Critics of non-directivity might present extreme hypothetical situations in an attempt to defeat the construct. However, 'hard cases make bad law' and no sensible *general* practice can be based on the *most unlikely* of circumstances. Others (e.g. Ellingham, 2005) complain that the concept of non-directivity lacks an agreed definition. Psychotherapy would be very thin on concepts if all the inexactly defined, contentious ones were rejected! Indeed, yet others believe that the very plurality of psychotherapy theory, even within the boundaries of particular approaches, is one of its strengths.

Furthermore, Brodley carefully explains that non-directivity should not be confused with *influence*. It is clear that the simple fact of being in relationship with the counsellor will influence the client. Moreover, the professional counselling relationship is a relationship with the *aim* of change, and the energy for that change has to come from somewhere. If the client could change entirely on their own there would be no need for a therapeutic relationship. As Barbara Brodley writes: 'all therapists *influence* their clients. The universal goal of therapy is to influence clients towards growth and healing' (Brodley, 1999/2005: 1). Non-directive practice pursues the aim of influence on the client's own terms, without interfering to shape the client's work in accord with the counsellor's preferences, opinions, tastes or professional requirements.

Principled and instrumental non-directivity

The terms 'principled' and 'instrumental', when applied to non-directivity, were introduced by Barry Grant (1990/2002). Grant described two types or styles of non-directivity: one was *principled* in that the non-directivity originates from the counsellor's deeply held values. It is a spontaneous non-systematic (not part of a therapeutic 'plan') attitude of non-interference and ethical respect. It is not a defensive repertoire of 'hands off' behaviour, nor is it a ploy or technique for 'use' in the early stages of a counselling relationship aimed at building trust or a therapeutic alliance.

An *instrumental* style of non-directivity is where it is seen as a set of behaviours to be applied in an interview with a particular end in mind. In other words, using it like a tool or instrument, as I mentioned above, for example, to foster a sense of trust in the client. However, such a use would seem to me, at least, to be self-defeating. Surely clients would be offended if they learned that their feelings of trust in the therapist had been *manipulated* by the application of a tool or technique, rather than originating in the character of the counsellor?

Grant sees principled non-directivity as a quality that only finds expression through the therapist-provided conditions of empathy, UPR and congruence, and the whole piece constitutes a set of praiseworthy human characteristics, quite apart from any therapeutic value they may have. It has been important for classical non-directive client-centred therapists to distinguish their theory and practice from the more INTEGRATIVE types of practice which see therapeutic conditions as skills or competencies to be applied as the situation demands. It is apparent this understanding of non-directivity goes hand in hand with the antidiagnostic stance of the classical practitioner, since to *use* any condition as a response to a particular situation requires the counsellor to diagnose the situation and see whether the condition is appropriate. It is not uncommon to hear some INTEGRATIVE practitioners declare that they 'used' empathy, or congruence or UPR. This would be a philosophical *and* a therapeutic mistake as far as classical client-centred therapy is concerned.

WHY BE NON-DIRECTIVE?

Although some people say that values of ethical living are enough to justify principled non-directivity (Grant, 2004, 2005; Schmid, 2005), there are theoretical arguments for the therapeutic benefits of non-directivity. In Chapter 7 (UPR) and Chapter 9 (The Client Feels Understood and Accepted) I used Proposition 17 (Rogers 1951: 517) to explain the change moment in person-centred theory:

> XVII) Under certain conditions, involving primarily complete absence of any threat to the self structure, experiences which are inconsistent with it may be perceived and examined, and the structure of the self revised to assimilate and include such experiences. (Ibid.)

If a non-threatening relationship is our goal, some theorists suggest that a relationship in which the counsellor does not direct the content or the process of the session would be preferable to one in which the counsellor proffers advice and instructions from an expert position—in which the counsellor tells the client what is wrong with them and what to do about it. Others point out that many clients find it reassuring to be told what to do. Indeed some clients feel quite disturbed when a counsellor *fails* to act like the expert they expect her to be.

The classical client-centred position on this is both quite clear and based in theory. Whilst it *is* true that what is threatening or not is a matter of each individual person's psychology; some clients *are* terrified of warm unconditional acceptance and the freedom to decide for themselves. However, counsellors that behave like experts or alleviate the client's anxiety by directing the session are colluding with an INTROJECTION (see pp. 59–60 and Chapter 11).

One of the aims of person-centred counselling is to help the client move their LOCUS OF CONTROL from outside (when they were dependent on other people for advice and direction to make decisions in their lives) to the inside (when they make decisions for themselves). Non-directivity is one of the ingredients of person-centred counselling which works towards this goal in that the counsellor refuses to make decisions for the client, even down to choosing topics for discussion in the counselling session, or making suggestions about how the client might think or behave.

It follows from the above that non-directivity is an attitude that fosters self-sufficiency and works against the client becoming dependent upon the counsellor. It also requires the counsellor to be constantly reviewing the issue of power in the counselling relationship. In a formal helping relationship nothing can remove the structural power imbalance between the helper and the person being helped, but a commitment to non-directivity helps keep the counsellor's awareness of power dynamics high.

The final theoretical justification for this (and last word on the subject in this chapter) lies in the person-centred understanding of the actualising tendency as a socially constructive forward-moving disposition. It challenges the notion (implicit in the 'expertise' of the counsellor) that:

> the individual ... cannot be trusted—that he must be guided, instructed, rewarded, punished and controlled by those who are higher in status. (Rogers, 1978: 8)

11

THE PROCESS OF CHANGE

This subheading is taken from the title of Chapter 7 in *On Becoming a Person*, (Rogers, 1961) and sprang from work done with Eugene Gendlin on the 'WISCONSIN PROJECT' (Rogers, Gendlin, Kiesler & Truax, 1967). However, it is clear that for many years Rogers had been interested in how change happens and what it means for the person to change, since he devoted a whole section (four chapters) to it in his 1942 book *Counseling and Psychotherapy*.

I chose to recall the title from Rogers' 1961 work for this chapter because it signalled a new understanding of the concept of change. Both PSYCHOANALYTIC and BEHAVIOURAL approaches to therapy saw change as the dismantling of a 'faulty' personality and rebuilding it 'correctly', i.e. that personality was a *structure* within the person, and could, in simple terms, have poor foundations or weak walls, whilst others thought it was all a matter of faulty learning—like computer programming with bugs which could be de-bugged and reprogrammed. Rogers (influenced by Gendlin) saw both personality *and* change as differences in the ways that experiences were apprehended and realised within the organism.

These different ways of understanding personality and change are important. They affect everything we do in therapy in that person-centred counselling doesn't try to *cure* an *illness*, or even *mend* something that is *broken*. Rather we try to facilitate a process of *growth* already inherent in the organism. What makes the growth better as a result of counselling are the therapeutic conditions provided by the counsellor in person-centred practice.

As with so many of the 'revolutionary' aspects of what Rogers called his 'new approach' back in the 1940s, twenty-first century readers might not find these ways of thinking too remarkable. It is important to realise, however, that this way of thinking fundamentally changes the nature of the whole helping enterprise.

One of the many consequences is that person-centred counselling does not fit in to the 'illness-diagnosis-treatment-cure' MEDICAL MODEL (see Chapter 5 for more detail on this). There is a continuing problem with this position in that the world of psychotherapy and counselling in the USA and the UK is increasingly influenced by and dependent upon the medical profession. Classical person-centred counselling finds itself increasingly marginalised as a result (see Chapter 14, pp. 103–4)

Another consequence is that person-centred theory is presenting a view ('process' rather than 'structure') that is increasingly counter-cultural. In the twenty-first century, it would appear that people feel more comfortable if responsibility for personal distress is located, by medical diagnosis, in the physiological (a 'chemical imbalance') or genetic (the 'SCHIZOPHRENIA gene') domains. Person-centred theory continues to be quite consciously out of step with many in the helping professions by asserting, for example, that 'depression' is not an illness, nor is it caused by faulty neurology, a chemical imbalance, an inherited gene, or bad learning. Person-centred theory has it caused by unfavourable conditions, both interpersonal and environmental.

The seven stages of process

Since person-centred theory contends that personality is a process, then it follows that the change event is also a process, not moving from a broken state to a fixed state, or from a 'sick' state to a 'healthy' state.

Rogers describes the process of change in seven stages. This is quite arbitrary—there is nothing implicit in the notion of stages or the number seven—it simply gives a structure to what would otherwise be a rather awkward description of a fluid process. Into these seven stages Rogers divides a number of dimensions of processing which I will summarise in a moment. First we need to know that when talking about movement along this continuum of process, Rogers condenses his six therapeutic conditions into one idea, namely 'that the client experiences himself as being fully *received*' (Rogers, 1961: 130, original emphasis). Rogers explains:

> By this I mean that whatever his feelings—fear, despair, insecurity, anger, whatever his mode of expression—silence, gestures, tears, or words; whatever he finds himself being in this moment, he senses that he is psychologically *received*, just as he is, by the therapist. (Ibid.: 130–1, original emphasis)

So when the client feels that their experiences have been fully received by the counsellor the process of change is inevitable. The trick is to *be* in such a way that the client feels *fully received*. The process continuum is arranged between two polarised positions, one in which process is stuck, rigid and fixed, and the other in which it is completely fluid, flowing and adaptable.

For full details and examples of the snapshots of the process captured at each of the stages, see Rogers (1961: 132–55). Only a very brief summary is possible here of the dimensions of change which Rogers divided into seven stages:

Stage 1	Stage 2	Stage 3	Stage 4	Stage 5	Stage 6	Stage 7
process is so fixed and stuck that the person is unlikely to come for therapy—they think everyone else has a problem		⟹ process of change ⟹				process so spontaneous and fluid that almost continuous change happens outside the session as much as in the session

Feelings

The person moves from hardly recognising feelings at all, to describing feelings as objects in the past ('I was suffering from depression'), then tentatively acknowledging feelings, but being frightened of them, to fully experiencing feelings in the present. Feelings no longer are feared, nor do they feel 'stuck'. In the later stages, Rogers (1961) says that feelings flow to their full result, meaning that they don't get strangled or halted before the full expression leads to a feeling of being cleansed.

PERSONAL CONSTRUCTS

In stage one, ideas about the self are not even entertained. The person gradually becomes aware of PERSONAL CONSTRUCTS but only thinking of them as facts. Then at a key moment in stage 3, they are recognised, albeit rigidly, as ideas not facts, and therefore potentially changeable—so the client can now believe that change is possible. As self-related ideas become more and more acknowledged and flexible, the whole SELF-STRUCTURE becomes fluid and eventually open to being revised frequently.

Internal dialogue

The person starts off having little or no internal 'conversations' and being largely fearful of paying too much attention to him/herself ('you think too much'). As their fear of looking 'inside' at themselves lessens they slowly experiment until they are able to have almost constant, mostly comfortable, internal dialogue as a matter of course in daily life.

Expression

People in the early stages of process are largely inexpressive. They don't talk about themselves much and are embarrassed or nervous when doing so, thinking it is pointless. Loosening of their process leads to free expression, including expression of feelings. In addition, in the final stages, individuals welcome and trust this flow of expression.

Differentiation and elaboration of experience

Clients begin counselling seeing things (their experiences of others and themselves, moral issues, etc.) in highly contrasting, right/wrong categories—there are almost no 'grey areas'. As they begin to tease apart (differentiate) and see greater intricacy in (elaborate) all of their experiences of themselves, others and the world, they begin to see the complexity in experience. This leads to discovering diversity and plurality *in themselves*, amongst others and in the world. Eventually they not only experience this diversity and plurality without fear, they welcome it.

Perception of problems
People start off believing that they couldn't possibly have any problems. Everyone else has the problem, not them. They gradually begin to be able to look at and understand themselves (see PERSONAL CONSTRUCTS above) with less and less fear, eventually being comfortable with the idea that they are a mixture of lived possibilities, some of which they experience as positive, some as negative. None of which necessarily generate feelings of great fear.

Attitude to change
Where it was once denied even as a possibility, change becomes an accepted, welcome part of the process of living. Clients might start with a 'If it ain't broke, don't fix it' or 'a leopard can't change its spots' attitude, but end up relishing change as a challenge. Along the way, the client will move through times of being afraid of change to varying degrees, depending upon how central the focus of change is to their SELF-CONCEPT. The client remains open to change in the future as a result of getting to the later stages of this process.

Bodily changes
The psychological changes described above run alongside what Rogers (1961) described as 'physiological' changes. What he described included the increasing tendency to suffer from fewer bodily (embodied) symptoms of anxiety (headaches, irritability, digestive problems, etc.) on the one hand, and more physical manifestations of ease, contentedness and feeling at one with things and happy with oneself (muscular relaxation, bright eyes, free breathing, physical responsiveness).

The self-perpetuating nature of the change process
One feature of the process of change worthy of special note is how it takes on a life of its own part way through the trajectory of the change process. At the sixth stage, Rogers hypothesised that the change process became irreversible and unstoppable. In other words there was no 'going back' and the process would continue

whether or not the client visited a counsellor—it occurred as much outside the counselling session as inside it.

The idiosyncratic nature of the change process

Finally, a reminder to remember that these stages or phases are completely arbitrary markers that don't exist and never have done in any real person's change process. The process of change is unique in each case—an irregular, halting trajectory frequently of the three-steps-forward, two-steps-back variety, nor will it proceed at the same rate in all areas of a person's life.

Rogers wrote about it partly to help generate hypotheses for research, and counsellors might find it useful to retrospectively analyse a counselling relationship, or in supervision. Whilst we might recognise elements in our own experience or our understanding of others, we must resist any temptation to think about these stages when we are with a client.

WHAT DOES THE CLIENT BRING TO THE PARTY?

A welcome effect of the notion of the process of change is that it reminded person-centred theorists and practitioners that the name of the therapy used to be 'client'-centred. Some started to become more (we might say belatedly) interested in how the client takes an active part in the therapeutic process. The idea that the client actually *does* something (i.e. is an 'active self-healer') is often missing from books on therapy which seem to focus almost exclusively on what the counsellor is, or should be, doing.

Other therapeutic approaches, CBT (COGNITIVE BEHAVIOUR THERAPY) being a good example, take a very positive view of a client's 'coping strategies' and they specifically try to help the client enhance these as long as the client's existing strategies are not self- (or other-) destructive.

Person-centred practitioners have a 'default position' of understanding that the client *at least* has a tendency to actualise, to make the best of the prevailing circumstances. However some theorists sought a more detailed explanation.

Art Bohart (Bohart, 2004; Bohart & Tallman, 1999) collected

evidence that clients can make positive use of practically everything that happens in a counselling session, even what all observers agreed were 'poor' therapist responses. He suggests that they do two things in therapy to make it work for them:

1. They look beyond the superficial things (like individual therapist responses) for the underlying stable elements such as the attitudes and values of the therapist and the nature of the therapy process.

2. They look for things to make positive use of, which can be practically anything the therapist says or does, and might include suggestions or advice from the therapist (but the client will use everything in their own way, *regardless of what the therapist may have intended*).

Although these results suggest that even poor responses from the counsellor can be turned to positive effect by the client, they do not give licence for poor practice. It is clear that Bohart is explaining occasional *lapses* or *mistakes* rather than consistently bad counselling. The point for counsellors to take note of is that clients are not passive recipients of therapeutic conditions. They are active seekers of positive factors.

Furthermore, Bohart believes that this explains why clients get better even though they don't seem to be doing what the theories of therapy say they should be doing. He concludes that they are running their change process themselves according to their own rules. Client-centred indeed!

12

PERSON-CENTRED
COUNSELLING TRANSCRIPT

Counselling is not a spectator sport and so generally lacks drama. Most of the time it is the ordinary unfolding of a relationship in which, as Art Bohart noted, see pp. 91–2, *if* clients get better, they may do so by methods that frequently remain a mystery to their counsellors. So what follows is an *illustration* of what part of a first session might be like. It is person-centred, so you should see no 'techniques', no 'interpretations', no 'diagnosis' and not even any *deliberate* attempt by the counsellor to 'build a rapport'. What you should see is a consistent effort to understand and be genuine.

THE SETTING

… is a voluntary agency offering counselling services for young people, including a drop-in service. The volunteer counsellor is Jill—newly qualified with a diploma in counselling. She occasionally staffs the drop-in but has a few regular pre-booked sessions as well. The client introduces himself as Ram. It is the first time that Ram has seen Jill, although he has been to the drop-in a couple of times before. Jill spends the first couple of minutes explaining to Ram what the boundaries of the session will be, making an agreement with him about seeing him for what will probably be just the one session and what that entails. It is this CONTRACT that they arrange that makes their relationship 'counselling' rather than 'support' or the use of 'counselling skills'. She also explains that he could book more sessions and become her client at the agency, rather than taking his chance at the drop-in.

R1: I've seen Alf before and he knows all about me …
J1: Um hmm, you'd rather see Alf, I can see that, and you think that if you stay and talk to me you'll have to spend some time giving me a load of background information …
R2: … well, not a load, but …

J2:   Ok, not a load, but enough so I know something about what's going on for you, some, er, background.

R3:   Has Alf told you about me?

J3:   No. We do keep notes on clients and Alf will have written something about you, but I haven't seen it. Here at the drop-in we don't know who's coming, that's why it's, erm, well …

R4:   Called a drop-in, (both laugh), yes, I know I'm just being stupid. When I get wound up I get in a state, you know, can't think straight, get spaced …

J4:   You were wound up when you got here and you couldn't think straight. And you thought it would be best to not have to go through all the background stuff again … especially when you feel like this, is that what you mean Ram? That you feel wound up right now?

R5:   Sort of. What happened is this. I, erm, er … I, er (stares wide-eyed and shuffles around in seat), well, I mean, I, er …

J5:   Take your time, we've got almost an hour.

R6:   Yes, I, well, it's like this, I used to go out and get off my head, weed and speed you know depending on who I was with, like. (Looks hard at Jill.)

J6:   Um hmm.

R7:   Well, I get kind of jittery, shaky and all worked up.

J7:   Jittery, shaky, OK and I'm not sure I know what you mean by 'worked up'.

R8:   Well, shit-scared. It's scary. I feel … (tails off)

J8:   I see, you feel shit-scared and it's happened more than once.

R9:   Yes, right. At first I, well, Kisha like she lights up a spliff to calm me down because she looks at me funny and she says to come and sit down and have a smoke. But it doesn't help at all and I get up and start walking up and down, up and down.

J9:   You can't shake this off, and you keep pacing up and down, over and over, until it goes away, is that right?

R10: Right, right, and I, but am I going mad? Is it the speed or what they say on the telly about the weed making you go mad, is it that? Because I haven't touched the stuff for weeks now and I swear man it keeps happening, like if I get stressed, I'm shitting myself and I really do shit myself, like I have to crap like the shits man.

J10: You actually get the shits, you're that scared. And it's happened more than once … and oh and worse, more frightening still, you've not done any drugs for weeks and it's *still* happening.

R11:Right. Is that bad? I mean, can you …

J11: You asked before, 'Am I going mad?' It's really frightening you now because you've seen some things on TV about weed and mental illness, right?

R12:Right.

J12: And you want me to tell you if you're going mad.

R13:Yeah.

J13: OK Ram, well I don't know the answer to that question. It would be great if I did and could say, one way or the other, but, erm, I would be guessing. We have a leaflet outside about …

R14: Oh, I thought you'd know, do you know? I mean, would you tell me if you knew? Like am I mad, or … (gets agitated again)

J14: Ram, I can see how much this is really frightening you and how important it is to know. But I won't say something I don't know, or just to reassure you so you go away feeling OK for a while. What I can see is how scared you are and how when this happens you are, maybe more scared than you've ever been before, than you ever thought possible? And having an answer would be, would make you feel a whole lot better.

R15: Shit. Oh shit. Fuck, sorry, I mean oh fuck. I need someone to help me here. Then I think it serves me right, you know, 'cos I did some bad things.

J15: This really does get to you. That sounds really, erm, desperate 'I need someone help me here'. And you think somehow it's happening because you did bad things?

R16: I'm fine right now, well not fine, I mean, like I am *thinking* about it all and feeling scared, but when it comes, like it's a monster or something grips me like a real thing you know, not like I'm imagining it, but *real*. Really *real*. Actually happening to me. I shit myself. I would be up out of this chair and up and down or out of the room like, like I gotta get out of here.

J16: So you're only *thinking* or, erm, remembering it now, the way it grips you, like a beast or something coming over you, real and terrifying, taking you over so you have to just get out and …

R17: Escape … no, you're right, *walk*. Walking helps I think. Walking up and down or just walking along. If it comes, I get out of the flat and walk. In the rain, or at night, just walk. Even my work don't help (surprised), just walking.

J17: So walking gives you respite or, not quite control over it, but helps take the edge off it. And you sounded surprised that work doesn't help.

R18: Yeah, I just thought why walking? Why not something really important like Kisha or my work, man? My work, it's supposed to do that, you know?

J19: This fear seems more likely to be beaten by something everyday like walking. Not something that means more to you, like Kisha or your work. Your work sounds really important to you. What work do you do?

R20: Well I call it my work, but it's not my job, like, I drive a van for my uncle, but my *work*, like what I am *supposed* to do, you know, what I am here for is, erm, don't laugh, I don't tell no one, not much, I write words, lyrics … you'd call it poems.

J20: Although you earn money driving for your uncle, your *life's work*, like it gives meaning to your life, that's what I might call 'writing poetry'. And no-one knows about this?

R21: Well, I did try to tell my dad when I was, I dunno, younger, and I said I wanted to go to college to learn about it. Can you get a job doing that? He just said it was for women.

J21: Writing and poetry isn't a job for men, your dad says.

R22: No, he's old fashioned like that, but he's not bad, you know? Now what he *really* doesn't like is me living with Kisha but he hasn't killed me or anything. He doesn't ask about her or anything, cuts her out. But I can take it now … I don't tell no one about my work though. No.

J22: There is affection in your voice when you talk about your dad and at the same time you know he disapproves of you living with Kisha and thinks your poetry is for women.

WHAT WAS HAPPENING?

Ram stayed for the whole session, slowly getting more comfortable, talking more about his father and family. Before I point out one or two events which signal something about being person-centred, I hope it's not too irritating if I suggest that first you decide for yourself, or talk about it with fellow students.

First, notice that Jill is quite vocal. Being person-centred doesn't mean sitting back making 'um hmm' noises every few seconds. It is possible to communicate your effort to be empathic early on by reflection without interrupting the client's flow too much.

Second, Jill does her best to answer straightforward questions (R10 and J11). It is respectful to do so. When she doesn't know the answer she says so and at the same time tries to pick up any feelings or thoughts behind the question.

Third, as in most counselling approaches, much of the first session is taken up with hearing the client's story, but this is brought right into the 'here and now' because of his agitation and fear. This fear will make his SELF-STRUCTURE rigid and defended. Understanding and acceptance (not interpretation and judgement) are the keys.

Fourth, Jill follows Ram, rather than leading. It would have been easy for her to follow any curiosity she might have about the 'bad things' he says he has done. She reflects this back in J15, but leaves it when Ram doesn't go back to it. Maybe he will bring it up again later. This demonstrates how the client is in control.

Fourth, towards the end (R21 onwards) Ram talks about his father and hints at some INTROJECTED VALUES and CONDITIONS OF WORTH. Although this might be a key piece of theory-in-practice unfolding, again Jill doesn't *pursue* the theme, she continues to be empathic, non-judgemental and genuine. She follows what Ram is saying, what is important to *him*, not what Jill thinks might be important for him according to the theory.

Finally, although this cannot be shown, Jill found the interview with Ram challenging—he was agitated and anxious and described symptoms of acute anxiety. This was new territory for Jill. She talked it through with the senior counsellor on duty immediately afterwards and in her next supervision session.

13

APPLICATIONS OF
PERSON-CENTRED COUNSELLING

IN THE BEGINNING

Person-centred counselling started, as client-centred counselling, in the University of Chicago Counseling Center in the 1940s (see Kirschenbaum, 1979, 2007; Barrett-Lennard, 1998; Sanders, 2004 for historical accounts of varying length and nuance). The Center provided counselling for students at the university and members of the public. It ran research programmes (the first research into psychotherapy using wax disc recordings) and soon became an international centre of excellence for innovation in psychotherapy. With its emphasis on research, client-centred therapy became the first evidence-based approach, and it was applied in a number of helping contexts, psychological, medical and para-professional.

The approach expanded rapidly in the USA and then in Europe. The client-centred therapy star rose quickly and burned brightly for 20 years in the USA, only to fade just as rapidly when Rogers left academic life in the early 1960s. In that short time, however, it influenced the helping professions, from clinical psychology, through schools counselling to para-professionals and the voluntary sector in a wide range of settings.

EARLY PERSON-CENTRED WORK IN THE UNITED KINGDOM

In the UK, person-centred counselling (PCC) was popularised by the early work of the National Marriage Guidance Council (now Relate) in the late 1960s and early 1970s. Rogers' work also informed the handful of counselling courses available from the mid-1960s to the mid-1970s which trained people to work as counsellors in educational settings and enter the new careers of 'student counsellor' and 'school counsellor' (springing out of demand for something extra from careers services in universities and schools respectively). A succession of American visiting professors to courses at the universities of Keele, Reading and Aston brought Rogers' ideas to the UK[1] and many of the new university counselling services offered PCC. These services were usually generic; meaning that they offered support across a wide range of student problems, from careers advice and study-skills advice through to therapeutic counselling. The services were, in every sense, student-centred.

The Facilitator Development Institute (FDI), inaugurated in 1975, also become a major focus of activity and training for those interested in Rogers' work (Thorne & Lambers, 1998). FDI alumni came from a very wide variety of helping and other occupational backgrounds and took Rogers' ideas back to their places of work.

What we know now as the 'voluntary sector' included a small number of counselling services, mainly for young people. From the mid-1970s, the National Association of Young People's Counselling and Advisory Services (NAYPCAS: now Youth Access) did more or less as its name suggests and person-centred counselling (by volunteers with anything from 15–100 hours' training) was offered by many services which came under its umbrella.

It isn't possible or necessary to give a complete account of the history of person-centred counselling in the UK in order to convey the very simple and powerful truth that many of us know from personal experience—that Rogers' work influences and changes people more-or-less on contact. Engagement with the values and principles at the heart of the PCA enthuses people to the extent that they almost immediately start to creatively apply the principles to their own life and work. So the approach spread to just about every person-to-person helping situation imaginable.

COUNSELLING AND/OR PSYCHOTHERAPY

Because of the history of the development of the helping professions

---

1. The UK lagged behind other European countries in its engagement with client/person-centred therapy—e.g. in the Netherlands and Belgium interest was building as early as the 1950s (see Thorne & Lambers, 1998). Crucially, interest in the UK was developed in the counselling and advisory sector in education, *not* in clinical psychology or psychotherapy which remained dominated by measurement, testing and PSYCHODYNAMIC therapies respectively.

in the UK, there continues to be a debate regarding whether there is any difference between counselling and psychotherapy, other than salary as mischievously pointed out by Windy Dryden. A quick search of the Internet will yield much food for thought.

It was Carl Rogers who first coined the term 'counselling' for the kind of helping work described in this book. When at the University of Chicago, psychiatrists objected to Rogers' use of the term 'psychotherapy' to describe the work he, his colleagues and students were doing on the grounds that 'psychotherapy' could only be practised by medically qualified people (psychiatrists). So what started as a contentious issue continues to be so. Client-centred therapists could see no difference in the activities in the late 1940s and person-centred practitioners see no difference today. (See Thorne, 1992, 1999 for discussion of the issues.)

RECENT AND CURRENT APPLICATIONS IN THE UK

Person-centred counselling (PCC) has a very wide range of applications by virtue of the universality of its theory and the fact that it is based on the core relationship elements of understanding, respect and genuineness. There are practically no helping settings where these elements are *not* useful and effective (see Chapter 14), and the range of activities of the members of the British Association for the Person-Centred Approach (BAPCA) is further testimony to this. I offer a selection of settings for consideration.

PRIMARY CARE PCC is probably the most common approach offered in GP surgeries in the UK, and it is also the most popular with patients (King et al., 2000).

SECONDARY CARE PCC is offered in many specialist care services as patient support and counselling (e.g. IVF services, transplant services, etc.).

DRUG AND ALCOHOL REHABILITATION Although CBT is favoured by service managers, PCC is offered in many places. It is not popular with funding bodies because it is not problem-oriented but nevertheless it is popular with clients (see Bryant-Jefferies, 2001).

PSYCHIATRIC CARE PCC is practised in psychiatric in- and out-patient care in pockets in the UK and mainland Europe. It has been suggested that PCC is not suitable for people who have a diagnosis of 'PSYCHOSIS' but radical psychologists and psychiatrists e.g. Breggin (1993) and Mosher (Mosher & Hendrix, 2004) describe treatments that to all intents and purposes *are* person-centred. For person-centred work in psychiatric care, see Sommerbeck, 2003; Freeth, 2007.

STUDENT COUNSELLING PCC continues to be popular and influential in further and higher education counselling.

SCHOOLS COUNSELLING Although something of a political football, schools counselling is enjoying a renaissance and PCC is well represented, see the Strathclyde University *Counselling in Schools Project: Evaluation Report.*

SPIRITUALITY PCC has been associated with several spiritual traditions including: Buddhism (Purton, 1996), Christianity (Thorne, 1998), Taoism (Miller, 1998) and generally encouraged in the UK by the work of Brian Thorne (1985, 1991, 1998).

CHILDREN Virginia Axline, one of Rogers' early doctoral students, is well known for popularising a non-directive approach to play therapy (Axline, 1964). Training opportunities are practically nonexistent in the UK but PCC is offered in private practice (see Keys & Walshaw, 2008).

COUPLES Although Relate now promotes an INTEGRATIVE model, PCC is widely offered to couples by private practitioners. See O'Leary (1999) for theory and practice. PCC is also a good basis for mediation.

FAMILIES Statutory services are dominated by systemic approaches, (and still not widely available) but PCC is offered by some private practitioners. See Gaylin (2001) for theory and practice.

VOLUNTARY WORK PCC is extensively available in the voluntary sector in young people's counselling services (some of which are active in developing theory and practice, see, e.g. Spandler, 1996; Keys & Walshaw, 2008). PCC is also well represented in a wider range of services, e.g. for asylum seekers, refugees and victims of torture, see e.g. Boyles, 2006.

This is not a comprehensive list of applications of PCC in the UK, but it serves as an illustration of the range of possibilities. For more information, readers are directed to BAPCA (see page 109), and new applications continue to emerge.

14

RESEARCH INTO
PERSON-CENTRED COUNSELLING

PETE SANDERS AND MICK COOPER

Only a few years ago, this would probably have been the chapter that most readers avoided. Nowadays, since the rise of interest in 'evidence-based practice', whilst it is unlikely that it will be the first chapter turned to, it is more than likely that it will at least get read. Our look at research will be brief and starts with a historical perspective that some readers might find surprising.

IN THE BEGINNING

> … for developing an original method to objectify the description and analysis of the psychotherapeutic process, for formulating a testable theory of psychotherapy and its effects on personality and behavior, and for extensive systematic research to exhibit the value of the method and explore and test the implications of the theory. His … flexible adaptation of scientific method in his attack on the formidable problems involved in the modification of the individual person *have moved this area of psychological interest within the boundaries of scientific psychology.* (Kirschenbaum & Henderson, 1990: 201, my emphasis)

Although many readers might imagine that evidence-based practice is a twenty-first century invention, and that it might be the practically exclusive domain of COGNITIVE BEHAVIOUR THERAPIES, history shows us that the original evidence-based work was done by Carl Rogers. The quote is part of the citation for the first ever Distinguished Scientific Contribution Award presented by the American Psychological Association to Carl Rogers in 1956.

Carl Rogers and his associates were the first to publish[1] full transcripts of therapy sessions,[2] using the then new technology of wax disc recordings. They were the first to attempt to subject these

---

1. Although a transcript of a complete psychoanalysis had been made in 1935, it had not been published. [Footnote 2 opposite.]

and other data to *scientific* analysis (see Raskin, 2004). From the late 1940s to the mid 1950s, the University of Chicago Counseling Center was a world centre of excellence in psychotherapy research.

If we fast-forward to the early twenty-first century, we find very little research into psychotherapy OUTCOMES involving client-centred or person-centred therapy. Whilst there is not the space to detail the intervening events, they constitute such an important context for understanding the current state of research in psychotherapy that readers wishing to continue their studies in counselling to professional level are directed to Sanders (2004), for a brief account, or Barrett-Lennard (1998) for a more full account and Kirschenbaum (2007) for the best account.

DOES PERSON-CENTRED COUNSELLING WORK?

A word or two about research and a problem

Before we get to the results, it is important to understand something about research. In many places in our culture, research in psychology is presented as scientific. From its early days in the nineteenth century, psychologists thought that psychology's best chance of gaining credibility was to separate itself from philosophy and become more like the physical sciences. So they set about measuring things and counting things just like physicists and biologists, etc. Quite naturally this led to thinking that human beings not only were 'living machines' but that human mental life, 'the mind' was amenable to counting, measurement, and machine metaphors.

It pretty soon became clear that counting and measurement, when applied to the mind and human experience, was incredibly difficult and the results were highly variable—in fact hardly any two scientific psychologists could get the same measurements on anything. If the truth is revealed by scientific analysis, then quantifying the mind and human experience was proving difficult.

Two innovations proved interesting. One was the physical/ natural sciences method of dividing the things you are looking at

---

2. Eight complete sessions were published in Rogers' 1942 book *Counseling and Psychotherapy* as 'The Case of Herbert Bryan'.

into smaller and smaller units until you were at a level where things actually *did* provide RELIABLE measurements. This is called REDUCTIONISM. The second was to insist that scientific psychology should stick to the observable and measurable events in human life, i.e. behaviour. Descriptions of experiences, feelings and such like were not admissible. This was the basis of BEHAVIOURISM.

There were problems with REDUCTIONISM and BEHAVIOURISM. After a while people (even psychologists) thought that the research was demeaning (they didn't like being thought of as, and treated like, machines) and ridiculous (some research involved measuring extremely esoteric factors far removed from human everyday experience). This gave rise to HUMANISTIC PSYCHOLOGY which in turn revived interest in researching the *qualities* of human experience rather than the *quantities* of human behaviour (hence the terms QUALITATIVE and QUANTITATIVE research).

If you have read the rest of this book, you should be able to guess that person-centred psychology finds itself better suited to QUALITATIVE research. The problem is that since counselling is associated with a medical metaphor, medical-style research which looks at counselling as a 'cure' for an 'illness' or a 'fix' for something 'broken', is seen as the only sort of useful study and so RANDOMISED CONTROLLED TRIALS (RCTs: a QUANTITATIVE method) are required by NICE (National Institute for Health and Clinical Excellence) in order to sanction a 'treatment'.

Because of this philosophical difference, there have been few RCTs done on person-centred counselling and little funding has been provided. Nevertheless, the recent research which *does* involve person-centred therapies is very encouraging.

Contemporary evidence from several angles
1. OUTCOME studies (how clients feel at the end of counselling)
Recent extensive and rigorous 'meta-analyses' (i.e. analyses of findings from multiple studies) of client-centred/non-directive therapy (Elliott, Greenberg & Lietaer, 2004) found:
  • large difference between pre- and post-therapy 'effect size'
  • medium to large 'treatment' against 'control' effect size

The conclusion is that a significant proportion of clients improve following person-centred therapy, as compared with being on a waiting list or not having any therapy.

2. Comparative studies (comparing PCT with other approaches)
Elliott et al. (2004) found that client-centred therapy was inferior compared with COGNITIVE BEHAVIOUR THERAPY (CBT) and process-directive EXPERIENTIAL therapies but that these differences disappear when so-called 'researcher allegiance' (the bias given to the results when the researcher favours a particular approach) is removed. It is also true to say that OUTCOME MEASURES tend to favour more COGNITIVE-orientated and symptom-focused therapies.

There is a general and consistent finding across psychotherapy research literature that OUTCOMES of PCT (person-centred therapy) are equivalent to OUTCOMES of other therapies. This is the so-called 'Dodo bird' effect that different therapies bring about relatively similar degrees of psychological change (e.g. Lambert & Barley, 2002).

Michael King et al. (2000) published results of a highly rigorous RANDOMISED CONTROLLED TRIAL comparing non-directive counselling, CBT, and usual general practitioner care for patients with depression and mixed anxiety and depression in GP surgeries in London and Manchester. At 4 and 12 months there were no significant differences between OUTCOMES of CBT and non-directive therapy clients (and both were superior to usual GP care at 4 months, but not 12). Patient satisfaction data showed that patients preferred non-directive therapy to CBT.

The most recent study by Stiles et al. (2006) shows similar results, this time using CORE-OM (Clinical OUTCOMES in Routine Evaluation-OUTCOME Measure) data from 1309 patients. The data was collected over three years from 58 NHS sites. This means that the sample was fairly large and widespread, helping lessen any bias due to geographical location or type of service. They compared the OUTCOME data for CBT, PCT and PSYCHODYNAMIC therapy (PDT). Also of importance to the majority of readers of this book, the study uses UK data.

The study is not a RANDOMISED CONTROLLED TRIAL, but is significant nonetheless. The results showed:

- clients in all therapeutic approaches showed a 'marked improvement' (in research speak, this means STATISTICALLY SIGNIFICANT, or as near to 'proven' as you can get)
- in common with previous studies, there were no real differences between the approaches

This study shows more of the 'Dodo bird' effect, raising the question as to why CBT is frequently portrayed as the only suitable and/or effective psychological treatment. It also shows that psychological treatments *are* effective, although it cannot (because of lack of a control group) show that, in this case at least, the treatment was more effective than routine GP care or the waiting list.

You might then wonder why control groups aren't routine in research. First, they are very costly (note that I put this as the number one reason!); second, there are ethical reservations in that it would be inappropriate to withhold potentially beneficial treatment from people in the control group; and finally, just using people who agreed to be randomised (allocated by chance) might bias the results because such people might bring special qualities.

Finally, this study tentatively concluded that clients may actively manage their own therapy and the services provided in a way that tends to average out the effects of different approaches. We looked briefly at this idea in the work of Bohart and Tallman on page 91–2 (Bohart, 2004; Bohart & Tallman, 1999).

3. Effectiveness of PCT for different psychological problems
Despite the research results outlined above, evidence-based treatment guidelines for specific psychological 'disorders', such as the Department of Health's (2001) *Treatment Choices in Psychological Therapies and Counselling* (<www.dh.gov.uk/>) or the NICE clinical guidelines on depression (see <www.nice.org.uk/>) rarely cite PCT as an effective means of treating specific psychological problems. For instance: NICE's clinical guidelines on anxiety (December 2004) <www.nice. org.uk/page.aspx?o=cg022niceguideline> state:

> CBT should be used ... [and] delivered only by suitably trained and supervised people who can demonstrate that they adhere

> closely to empirically grounded treatment protocols … in the optimal
> range of duration (16–20 hours in total) … (p. 24)

The brief version of the DoH Guidelines (distributed to both GPs
and patients) makes no mention of 'person-centred therapy,'
subsuming it under 'counselling' which is described as:

> A form of psychological therapy that gives individuals an opportunity
> to explore, discover, and clarify ways of living more resourcefully,
> with a greater sense of well being. (p. 5)

The guidelines also state 'Patients who are adjusting to life events,
illnesses, disabilities or losses may benefit from brief therapies such
as counselling … There is evidence of counselling effectiveness in
mixed anxiety/depression, most effective when used with specific
client groups, e.g. postnatal mothers, bereaved groups' (pp. 3–4).
However, 'counselling' is not recommended as treatment for more
'serious' psychological problems, such as post-traumatic stress
disorder, anxiety, and eating disorders, whereas CBT is.

Nevertheless Elliott et al.'s (2004) review suggested that PCT
is as effective as CBT and process EXPERIENTIAL therapy with
anxiety disorders, depression, SCHIZOPHRENIA and severe, chronic
dysfunction when researcher allegiances are controlled for. Despite
this, there is widespread acknowledgement within the PCT
community of the urgent need to demonstrate effectiveness of
PCT with respect to specific psychological problems.

*4. Are the key ingredients of an effective therapeutic relationship
the same as Rogers' conditions?*
In 1999 the American Psychological Association Division of
Psychotherapy Task Force (see Norcross, 2002) was commissioned
to undertake the largest ever review of empirical study into
therapeutic relationship variables and their relationship to
therapeutic OUTCOMES. It concluded that:

- *Empathy* is one of three 'demonstrably effective' elements of
  therapeutic relationship.
- *Positive regard* and *congruence* were among seven 'promising
  and probably effective' elements of therapeutic relationship.

Are the 'core conditions' necessary and sufficient? The evidence suggests that it's not possible to make such broad generalisations, as different clients need very different things. However, for most clients, the core conditions are *probably* sufficient to bring about some degree of therapeutic personality change; and with some clients, are *probably* sufficient to bring about a great deal of change. Some degree of empathy is *probably* necessary for most clients to bring about some degree of therapeutic personality change; and positive regard and congruence are *probably* necessary to a minimal degree for most clients.

Meta-analyses (analysis of the results of many outcome studies) across the therapies suggest that 40% improvement is due to: client variables and EXTRATHERAPEUTIC FACTORS; 30% due to the therapeutic relationship; 15% to expectancy and hope; with only 15% due to technique and model factors. A meta-analysis of outcomes of person-centred and experiential therapies (including classical CCT) funded by BAPCA is ongoing at the University of Strathclyde and early indications are very positive. So, there is considerable and mounting evidence.

Summary

- For most clients, person-centred therapy brings about significant levels of psychological improvement, most clearly demonstrated in clients with mild to moderate depression, and those who are dealing with specific life issues.
- After thousands of studies, there is no convincing evidence that person-centred therapy is any less (or more) effective than other established forms of psychological therapy, whether in general or in relation to specific psychological problems.
- Empathy, positive regard and congruence are probably not necessary and sufficient for *all* clients to achieve positive therapeutic change; but a strong correlation seems to exist between levels of empathy and therapeutic OUTCOMES; and positive regard and congruence also show some correlation with clients' levels of improvement.
- Get interested and involved in research: 'The facts are friendly' (Rogers, 1961: 25).

APPENDIX

RESOURCES FOR LEARNING

ORGANISATIONS

World Association for Person-Centered and Experiential Psychotherapy and Counseling (WAPCEPC)
<www.pce-world.org>
British Association for the Person-Centred Approach (BAPCA)
<www.bapca.org.uk>
Association for the Development of the Person-Centered Approach

JOURNALS

Person-Centered and Experiential Psychotherapies   The quarterly journal of WAPCEPC (also sent to all BAPCA members as part of their subscription).
Person-Centered Journal   The annual journal of the Association for the Development of the Person-Centered Approach.

WEBSITES

In addition to the organisation websites above, there are some websites which are good 'portals' because they have many links to websites with substantial content regarding person-centred therapy. Since websites occasionally change their URL or simply disappear, I suggest you use this link which has details of over 60 useful sites for counsellors and psychologists, 18 of them person-centred, and the list is added to regularly:
<www.pccs-books.co.uk/page.php?xPage=links.html>

FURTHER READING

Readers will realise that there are hundreds of books and articles which may be of interest to them. If you feel overwhelmed by the sheer number of books available and you want some guidance, these are the books that *I* think are particularly useful and/or important which are up-to-date, in print and available. This is *not* a definitive list, especially since by the time you are reading this book, a few more will have appeared on the scene. They are in alphabetical order by author

The life and work of Carl Rogers
Kirschenbaum, H (2007) *The Life and Work of Carl Rogers.* Ross-on-Wye: PCCS Books.

To accompany or follow immediately after an 'intermediate' (certificate) course in person-centred therapy

Merry, T (1995) *Invitation to Person-Centred Psychology.* Ross-on-Wye: PCCS Books.

Merry, T (2002) *Learning and Being in Person-Centred Counselling.* Ross-on-Wye: PCCS Books.

Sanders, P (ed) (2004) *The Tribes of the Person-Centred Nation: An introduction to the schools of therapy associated with the person-centred approach.* Ross-on-Wye: PCCS Books.

Tolan, J (2003) *Skills in Person-Centred Counselling and Psychotherapy.* London: Sage.

Tudor, K & Merry, T (2002) *Dictionary of Person-Centred Psychology.* Ross-0n-Wye: PCCS Books.

For 'professional' (degree, diploma or Masters) courses in person-centred therapy

Embleton Tudor, L, Keemar, K, Tudor, K, Valentine, J & Worrall, M (2004) *The Person-Centred Approach: A contemporary introduction.* Basingstoke: Palgrave.

Joseph, S & Worsley, R (eds) (2005) *Person-Centred Psychopathology: A positive psychology of mental health.* Ross-on-Wye: PCCS Books.

Mearns, D (2003) *Developing Person-Centred Counselling.* London: Sage.

Mearns, D & Cooper, M (2005) *Working at Relational Depth in Counselling and Psychotherapy.* London: Sage.

Mearns, D & Thorne, B (2000) *Person-Centred Therapy Today.* London: Sage.

Tudor, K & Worrall, M (2006) *Person-Centred Therapy: A clinical philosophy.* Hove: Routledge.

Wyatt, G (Series Editor) (2001/2) *Rogers' Therapeutic Conditions. Volumes 1, 2, 3 & 4.* Ross-on-Wye: PCCS Books. (See references section under Wyatt, 2001; Haugh & Merry, 2001; Bozarth & Wilkins, 2001 and Wyatt & Sanders, 2002.)

Wilkins P (2003) *Person-Centred Therapy in Focus.* London: Sage.

For professional study in integrative or other approaches

Mearns, D (2003) *Developing Person-Centred Counselling.* London: Sage.

Merry, T (2002) *Learning and Being in Person-Centred Counselling.* Ross-on-Wye: PCCS Books.

Sanders, P (ed) (2004) *The Tribes of the Person-Centred Nation: An introduction to the schools of therapy associated with the person-centred approach.* Ross-on-Wye: PCCS Books.

Wyatt, G (Series Editor) (2001/2) *Rogers' Therapeutic Conditions. Volumes 1, 2, 3 & 4.* Ross-on-Wye: PCCS Books. (See references section under Wyatt, 2001; Haugh & Merry, 2001; Bozarth & Wilkins, 2001 and Wyatt & Sanders, 2002.)

GLOSSARY

ADAPTATION   A biological term meaning a change due to natural selection over a period of time to a feature (structural, physiological or behavioural) of an organism.

BEHAVIOURISM   A 'school' of objective psychology and philosophy which rejects subjective experience and consciousness. It states that the only relevant, valid psychological events are those which can be observed, i.e. behaviour.

COGNITIVE (COGNITION)   Knowing-related thought processes, as opposed to feeling-related or emotional processes.

COGNITIVE (COUNSELLING/BEHAVIOUR THERAPY)   A 'school' of counselling/therapy based on theories which derive from cognitive theory, i.e. place prime importance on rational thought processes.

CONDITIONS OF WORTH   Coined by Rogers (1959) to mean the conditions of value placed on you by someone else, e.g. 'In order to be loved by me you must sit still and be quiet and polite.'

CONFIGURATIONS (OF SELF)   A term coined by Dave Mearns (1999) referring to parts or dimensions of a person's self-structure. Mearns and Thorne (2000: 102) '… a coherent pattern of feelings, thoughts and preferred behavioural responses … within the Self.'

CONTRACT   An agreement between the helper and the client which determines the kind of helping relationship it will be. If it is to be a counselling relationship, the contracting establishes things like the level of confidentiality offered, number and length of sessions, complaints procedures, etc.

DEATH INSTINCT   (Also called 'Thanatos') From Freud, the counterpart of the life instinct (Libido). The two prime motives in Freudian theory, one towards self-gratification, the other towards self-destruction.

DENIAL (TO AWARENESS)   One of the processes by which the self-concept protects itself. Symbolisation of experience is stopped half way, just after the experience has been detected as threatening and just before it comes fully into consciousness. Partnered with DISTORTION (below).

DIALOGICAL (THERAPY)   Not so much a 'school' as the idea that therapy *is* dialogue, *is* relational. It is a deep acknowledgement of the potential made possible by the separateness of client and counsellor in every moment of meeting. Sometimes called 'encounter-oriented approach'.

DISTORTION   The counterpart of DENIAL as the other method of rendering threatening experiences 'safe' to the self-concept, e.g. 'I don't have a problem with alcohol, some can hold their drink and I feel more relaxed after I've had a few.'

DRIVE   The hypothetical energy which derives from a physiological state (e.g. food deprivation) and causes the organism to behave in a drive-related manner (food-seeking and food-consuming behaviour). Theoretical building block of motivation in so-called 'drive theories'.

EXPERIENTIAL (COUNSELLING)   Eclectic approach which sprang from Rogers' and Gendlin's work, incorporating elements of Gestalt therapy. (See Baker, 2004 for introduction.) The term is also used by Mahrer (2004) to describe his (unrelated) approach.

EXTRATHERAPEUTIC FACTORS   Almost anything outside of therapy, such as the client's personality characteristics, social conditions, economic status etc.

FOCUSING (-ORIENTED COUNSELLING)   An approach developed by Eugene Gendlin, one of Carl Rogers' students and colleagues, and based on the inner flow of experience. (See Purton, 2004a or b for introduction.)

HOMOEOSTASIS   A regulatory mechanism to keep physiological systems in balance. Equilibrium maintained by feedback, e.g. increased body temperature causes sweating which cools down the body and stops sweating reflex. Is also used to explain behaviour via DRIVE-reduction. Body needs food ⇨ hunger ⇨ eating ⇨ balance restored.

HUMANISTIC PSYCHOLOGY   A reaction to both BEHAVIOURISM and PSYCHO-ANALYSIS (and so dubbed the 'third force' in psychology since neither represented the healthy, growthful, creative *person*), founded by, amongst others, Rogers (1951) and Maslow (1954).

INDIVIDUALISM   A world-view emphasising the importance of the individual and self-reliance/determination over group/society. Opposite of 'collectivism'.

INTEGRATIVE (COUNSELLING)   Any approach which blends (integrates) features of other approaches at the level of theory or practice (assembling techniques). There are many types of integrative counselling and most are idiosyncratic. See Culley and Bond (2004), or for a more critical view, Worsley (2004).

INTERNAL FRAME OF REFERENCE   Viewpoint from the perspective of the individual concerned. Subjective. External frame of reference would be the objective viewpoint from outside of the person.

INTERVENTION   Strictly speaking it means 'interference' (to stop something: to intervene). Often used to mean counsellor-response. Not frequently used in person-centred circles, some practitioners preferring to use 'contribution'.

INTROJECTS/INTROJECTED VALUES   Introjection is the act of taking something in and incorporating it into one's psychological structure without modification *and* then believing it originated from inside. So a child who is told 'you're a bad girl' takes this judgement into her self-concept and believes it to be *her own judgement of herself.*

LOCUS OF EVALUATION/CONTROL   The 'site' of evaluating experiences or controlling behaviour—either inside the person (internal) or outside the person (external: usually another person or group, e.g. 'society').

MEDICAL MODEL (OF MENTAL 'ILLNESS')   The system used to understand and classify psychological distress in the Western world. Classification system based on the similarity of symptoms, *not* on cause-and-effect relationships (is *not* a disease model, although it looks like one). It mimics a medical model of physical disease—used by psychiatrists and majority of mental health professionals.

MOTIVATION   The (hypothetical) process which determines behaviour, i.e. answers the question '*why* do animals behave?'

ORGANIC CONDITION/DISEASE   A condition or illness with a physical/biological cause (rather than psychological), e.g. brain tumours are physical (organic) entities but symptoms can in some circumstances look like the symptoms of psychological distress (mood swings). Also, e.g. delirium (hallucinations and delusions) caused by fever.

ORGANISMIC VALUING PROCESS   A process intrinsic to the organism, which continually evaluates experience according to the actualising tendency. The organism itself decides whether a particular experience is good or bad without reference to introjected values.

OUTCOME (MEASURES)   The measure of how a client feels at the end of therapy against an external yardstick (an anxiety or 'adjustment' scale or other PSYCHOMETRIC TEST). Not the same as a 'change status' measure which looks at improvement.

PERSONAL CONSTRUCTS   Constructs (ideas) about one's self and immediate relationships. Also a term coined for more particular use by Kelly (1955).

PHARMACOLOGY (PSYCHO-)   The study of drugs in psychological functioning.

PHENOMENOLOGY   Approach to understanding and psychology where 'truth' or 'knowledge' comes from the perceptual field of the individual, rather than an external authority. Based on work of philosopher Edmund Husserl.

PRIMARY PREVENTION RESEARCH   Looking at the factors which predispose people to certain conditions/distress, such as social and environmental conditions, and personal characteristics and experiences.

PSYCHOANALYSIS/PSYCHOANALYTIC   School of psychology originated by and based on the work of Sigmund Freud.

PSYCHODYNAMIC (COUNSELLING)   derived from PSYCHOANALYSIS and the work of Freud and later psychoanalytic theorists, with unconscious processes at the heart of the work.

PSYCHOLOGICAL TENSION   Phrase used by Rogers (1951, 1959) to mean the fundamental factor underpinning all feelings of distress, such as anxiety, depression, etc. Stems from incongruence between self and experience.

PSYCHOMETRIC TESTS   Any test which purports to measure a psychological trait or characteristic, such as intelligence, adjustment, anxiety, etc. (Note the variables measured are all constructs, i.e. hypothetical.)

PSYCHOPATHOLOGY   The study or manifestation of mental (psychological) disorder (pathology). A term originating in the medicalisation of distress.

PSYCHOSIS/PSYCHOTIC   A MEDICAL-MODEL classification of severe distress characterised by loss of contact with reality and lack of insight (person doesn't think they are 'ill'). Types include SCHIZOPHRENIA, clinical depression, bipolar disorder. (See Bentall, 2004.)

QUALITATIVE (RESEARCH METHODS)   Concerned with the *qualities* of experience and human behaviour. (See McLeod, 2003 or Wilkins, in press.)

QUANTITATIVE (RESEARCH METHODS)   Concerned with the *quantities* of experience and human behaviour. (See McLeod, 2003 or Wilkins in press.)

RANDOMISED CONTROLLED TRIALS   Patients/clients are randomly (by chance) allocated to one of two groups, one 'treatment' group and one 'control' group. The treatment group receives the treatment under investigation, and the control group receives either no treatment or some standard default treatment.

REDUCTIONISM/REDUCTIONISTIC   The method of analysis where the subject under study is broken down into simpler and simpler areas and units. This increasing simplification of a complex subject is based on the idea that complex processes can be entirely explained by looking at their assumed components. Difficulties arise when applied to human psychology.

REFLEXIVE PRACTICE   Self-referent practice, or referring back to one's self. Practising in a way which acknowledges the person of the counsellor as a key instrument in the change process.

RELIABLE/RELIABILITY   Replicability. In research terms the chance of getting the same results again.

SCHIZOPHRENIA   Serious psychological distress or mental 'illness'. Classified in MEDICAL MODEL as 'PSYCHOSIS'. Many very distressing symptoms of confused, chaotic thoughts and feelings, delusions and hallucinations. (See Bentall, 2004.)

SELF-CONCEPT   The view one has of one's self—part of the personality. More fluid in a fully functioning person, more rigid in an incongruent person.

SELF-PSYCHOLOGY   Theories which put the self at the centre of the theory. Most associated as a single approach with Heinz Kohut (see Lee, 1991).

SELF-STRUCTURE   More-or-less self-explanatory. The personality structure incorporating the self and self-concept.

SHADOW (SIDE)   Most associated with Freud and Jung, meaning the supposed 'dark' side of human nature comprising basic, intrinsic self- and other-destructive urges. See also DEATH INSTINCT.

SOCIALISATION   The process by which an individual becomes inducted into society, learning the 'rules and regulations' of living in association with others, from how to conduct yourself in interpersonal relationships to obeying the laws of society.

STATISTICAL SIGNIFICANCE   A measure of the probability of something happening by chance. In simple terms it is used to mean that it is a *real* effect.

SYMBOLISATION   Bringing an experience into conscious awareness and giving it meaning. So pre-symbolic experience would be an experience which either is not yet in awareness and or has no fully developed meaning.

TRAITS   Inferred (not directly observable) components of personality, an aspect of character such as 'dependability' or 'persistence'.

TYPE   Collections of traits put together to form character or personality types. Both traits and types are 'constructs', i.e. theoretical/hypothetical.

WISCONSIN PROJECT   Extensive research project on the effects of therapy conducted at Mendota State Hospital on hospitalised schizophrenics devised by Rogers and several colleagues. Rogers was professor of psychology and psychiatry at the University of Wisconsin at the time. (See Rogers et al., 1967.)

WORKING ALLIANCE   An essential component of a therapeutic relationship from psychodynamic theory—shared goals and rapport between client and counsellor.

REFERENCES

Axline, V (1964) *Dibs:In Search of Self.* Harmondsworth: Penguin.

Allport, GW (1937) *Personality: A psychological interpretation.* New York: Henry Holt.

Baker, N (2004) Experiential person-centred therapy. In P Sanders (ed) *The Tribes of the Person-Centred Nation*: *An introduction to the schools of therapy associated with the person-centred approach.* Ross-on-Wye: PCCS Books, pp. 67–94.

Barrett-Lennard, GT (1962) Dimensions of therapist response as causal factors in therapeutic change. *Psychological Monographs 76* (43, whole no. 562).

Barrett-Lennard, GT (1998) *Carl Rogers' Helping System: Journey and substance.* London: Sage.

Barrett-Lennard, GT (2002) Perceptual variables of the helping relationship: A measuring system and its fruits. In G Wyatt & P Sanders (eds) *Rogers' Therapeutic Conditions, Volume 4: Contact and Perception.* Ross-on-Wye: PCCS Books, pp. 25–50.

Barrett-Lennard, GT (2003) *Steps on a Mindful Journey.* Ross-on-Wye: PCCS Books.

Barrett-Lennard, GT (2005) *Relationship at the Centre.* London: Whurr.

Baughan, R & Merry, T (2001) Empathy: An evolutionary/biological perspective. In S Haugh and T Merry (eds) *Rogers' Therapeutic Conditions, Volume 2: Empathy.* Ross-on-Wye: PCCS Books, pp. 230–9.

Bentall, R (2004) *Madness Explained: Psychosis and human nature.* Harmondsworth: Penguin.

Bohart, AC (2004) How do clients make empathy work? *Person-Centered & Experiential Psychotherapies, 3* (2), 102–16.

Bohart, AC & Greenberg, LS (eds) (1997) *Empathy Reconsidered: New directions in psychotherapy.* Washington, DC: American Psychological Association.

Bohart, AC & Tallman, K (1999) *How Clients Make Therapy Work: The process of active self-healing.* Washington: American Psychological Association.

Bowlby, J (1953) *Child Care and the Growth of Love.* Harmondsworth: Pelican.

Boy, AV (1989/2002) Psychodiagnosis: A person-centered perspective. *Person-Centered Review, 4* (2), 132–51. Reprinted in D Cain (ed) (2002) *Classics in the Person-Centered Approach.* Ross-on-Wye: PCCS Books, pp. 385–96.

Boyles, J (2006) Not just naming the injustice—Counselling asylum seekers and refugees. In G Proctor, M Cooper, P Sanders & B Malcolm (eds) *Politicizing the Person-Centred Approach: An agenda for social change.* Ross-on-Wye: PCCS Books, pp. 156–66.

Bozarth JD (1984/2001) Beyond Reflection: Emergent modes of empathy. In JM Shlien & RF Levant (eds) *Client-Centered Therapy and the Person-Centered Approach.* Westport, CT: Praeger, pp. 59–75. Reprinted in S Haugh and T Merry (eds) *Rogers' Therapeutic Conditions, Volume 2: Empathy.* Ross-on-Wye: PCCS Books, pp. 131–43.

Bozarth, JD (1998) *Person-Centered Therapy: A revolutionary paradigm.*

Ross-on-Wye: PCCS Books.

Bozarth, J & Wilkins, P (2001) *Rogers' Therapeutic Conditions. Volume 2: Unconditional Positive Regard*. Ross-on-Wye: PCCS Books.

Breggin, P (1993) *Toxic Psychiatry*. London: HarperCollins.

Brodley, BT (1999/2005) About the non-directive attitude. *Person-Centred Practice*, 7 (2), 79–82. Reprinted in BE Levitt (ed) (2005) *Embracing Non-directivity*. Ross-on-Wye: PCCS Books, pp. 1–4.

Brodley BT (2002) Observations of empathic understanding in two client-centered therapists. In JC Watson, RN Goldman and MS Warner (eds) *Client-Centered and Experiential Psychotherapy in the 21st Century*. Ross-on-Wye: PCCS Books, pp. 182–203.

Bryant-Jefferies, R (2001) *Counselling the Person Beyond the Alcohol Problem*. London: Jessica Kingsley.

Cameron, R (2004) Psychological contact (Chapters 7 & 8). In J Tolan *Skills in Person-Centred Counselling and Psychotherapy*. London: Sage, pp. 87–109.

Coffeng, T (2002) Contact in the Therapy of Trauma and Dissociation. In G Wyatt & P Sanders (eds) *Rogers' Therapeutic Conditions, Volume 4: Contact and Perception*. Ross-on-Wye: PCCS Books, pp. 153–67.

Combs, AW & Snygg, D (1959) *Individual behavior: A perceptual approach to behavior*. New York: Harper and Row.

Cooper, M (2001) Embodied empathy. In S Haugh and T Merry (eds) (2001) *Rogers' Therapeutic Conditions, Volume 2: Empathy*. Ross-on-Wye: PCCS Books, pp. 218–29.

Culley, S & Bond, T (2004) *Integrative Counselling in Action* (2nd edn). London: Sage.

Davies, E & Burdett, J (2004) Preventing 'schizophrenia': Creating the conditions for saner societies. In J Read, LR Mosher & RP Bentall (eds) *Models of Madness: Psychological, social and biological approaches to schizophrenia*. London: Routledge, pp. 271–82.

Davies, N & Aykroyd, M (2002) Sexual orientation and psychological contact. In G Wyatt and P Sanders (eds) *Rogers' Therapeutic Conditions, Volume 4: Contact and Perception*. Ross-on-Wye: PCCS Books, pp. 221–33.

Ellingham, I (2005) Breaking free from non-directivity. *Therapy Today*, 16(10), 30.

Elliott, R, Greenberg, LS & Lietaer, G (2004) Research on experiential therapies. In MJ Lambert (ed) *Bergin and Garfield's Handbook of Psychotherapy and Behaviour Change*. Chicago: Wiley, pp. 493–539.

Embleton Tudor, L, Keemar, K, Tudor, K, Valentine, J, & Worrall, M (2004) *The Person-Centred Approach: A contemporary introduction*. Basingstoke: Palgrave.

Evans, R (1975) *Carl Rogers: The man and his ideas*. New York: Dutton.

Frankel, M & Sommerbeck, L (2005) Two Rogers and congruence: The emergence of therapist-centered therapy and the demise of client-centered therapy. In BE Levitt *Embracing Non-directivity*. Ross-on-Wye: PCCS Books, pp. 40–61.

Freeth, R (2007) *Humanising Psychiatry and Mental Health Care: The challenge of the person-centred approach*. Oxford: Radcliffe.

Gaylin, N (2001) *Family, Self and Psychotherapy: A person-centred perspective.* Ross-on-Wye: PCCS Books.

Grant, B (1990/2002) Principled and instrumental nondirectiveness in person-centered and client-centered therapy. *Person-Centered Review, 5* (1), 77–88. Reprinted in D Cain (ed) (2002) *Classics in the Person-Centered Approach.* Ross-on-Wye: PCCS Books, pp. 371–6.

Grant, B (2004) The imperative of ethical justification in psychotherapy: The special case of client-centered therapy. *Person-Centered & Experiential Psychotherapies, 3* (3), 152–65.

Grant, B (2005) Taking only what is given: Self-determination and empathy in non-directive client-centered psychotherapy. In BE Levitt (ed) *Embracing Non-directivity.* Ross-on-Wye: PCCS Books, pp. 248–60.

Harlow, HF (1959) Love in infant monkeys. *Scientific American, 200* (6), 68–74.

Haugh, S (2001) The difficulties in the conceptualisation of congruence: A way forward with complexity theory? In G Wyatt (ed) *Rogers' Therapeutic Conditions, Volume 1: Congruence.* Ross-on-Wye: PCCS Books, pp. 116–30.

Haugh, S & Merry, T (eds) (2001) *Rogers' Therapeutic Conditions, Volume 2: Empathy.* Ross-on-Wye: PCCS Books.

Joseph, S & Worsley, R (eds) (2005) *Person-Centred Psychopathology: A positive psychology of mental health.* Ross-on-Wye: PCCS Books.

Kelly GA (1955) *The Psychology of Personal Constructs, Volumes 1 and 2.* New York: Norton.

Keys, S & Walshaw, T (2008) *Person-Centred Work with Children and Young People: UK practitioner perspectives.* Ross-on-Wye: PCCS Books.

King, M, Sibbald, B, Ward, E, Bower, P, Lloyd, M, Gabbay, M & Byford, S (2000) Randomised control trial of non-directive counselling, cognitive-behaviour therapy and usual general practitioner care in the management of depression as well as mixed anxiety and depression in primary care. *Health Technology Assessment, 4* (19).

Kirschenbaum, H (1979) *On Becoming Carl Rogers.* New York: Delacorte.

Kirschenbaum, H (2007) *The Life and Work of Carl Rogers.* Ross-on-Wye: PCCS Books.

Kirschenbaum, H & Henderson, VL (1990) *The Carl Rogers Reader.* London: Constable.

Lambers, E (2003) Chapters 25, 26, 27 & 28. In D Mearns *Developing Person-Centred Counselling* (2nd edn). London: Sage, pp. 103–19.

Lambert MJ & Barley DE (2002) Research summary on the therapeutic relationship and psychotherapy outcome. In JC Norcross (ed) *Psychotherapy Relationships that Work: Therapist contributions and responsiveness to patients.* Oxford: Oxford University Press, pp. 17–32.

Lee, RR (1991) *Psychotherapy after Kohut: A textbook of self-psychology.* Hillsdale, NJ: Analytic Press.

Lietaer, G (1993/2001) Being genuine as a therapist: Congruence and transparency. In D Brazier (ed) *Beyond Carl Rogers.* London: Constable, pp. 17–46. Reprinted in G Wyatt (ed) *Rogers' Therapeutic Conditions, Volume 1: Congruence*. Ross-on-Wye: PCCS Books, pp. 36–54.

McLeod J (2003) *Doing Counselling Research* (2nd edn). London: Sage.

Mahrer, A (2004) *The Complete Guide to Experiential Psychotherapy.* Boulder, CO: Bull Publishing.

Maslow, A (1954) *Motivation and Personality*. New York: Harper.

Masson, J (1992) *Against Therapy.* London: Fontana.

Mearns, D (1996) Working in relational depth with clients in person-centred therapy. *Counselling, 7* (4), 306–11.

Mearns, D (1999) Person-centred therapy with configurations of the self. *Counselling, 10* (2), 125–30.

Mearns, D (2003) *Developing Person-Centred Counselling*. London: Sage.

Mearns, D & Cooper, M (2005) *Working at Relational Depth in Counselling and Psychotherapy.* London: Sage.

Mearns, D & Thorne, B (2000) *Person-Centred Therapy Today.* London: Sage.

Merry, T (1995) *Invitation to Person-Centred Psychology.* Ross-on-Wye: PCCS Books.

Merry, T (2002) *Learning and Being in Person-Centred Counselling.* Ross-on-Wye: PCCS Books.

Merry, T (2004) Classical client-centred therapy. In P Sanders (ed) *The Tribes of the Person-Centred Nation: An introduction to the schools of therapy associated with the person-centred approach.* Ross-on-Wye: PCCS Books, pp. 21–44.

Miller, MJ (1998) Some comparisons between Taoism and person-centered therapy. *The Person-Centered Journal, 3* (1), 12–14.

Moodley, R, Lago C & Talahite, A (2004) *Carl Rogers Counsels a Black Client: Race and culture in person-centred counselling.* Ross-on-Wye: PCCS Books.

Mosher, L & Hendrix, V (2004) *Soteria: Through madness to deliverence.* Philadelphia, PA: Xlibris.

Murphy, LJ & Mitchell, DL (1998) When writing helps to heal: E-mail as therapy. *British Journal of Guidance and Counselling, 26* (1), 21–32.

Norcross, JC (ed) (2002) *Psychotherapy Relationships that Work: Therapists contributions and responsiveness to patients.* New York: Oxford University Press.

O'Leary, C (1999) *Counselling Couples and Families: A person-centred approach.* London: Sage.

Proctor, G & Napier, MB (2004) *Encountering Feminism: Intersections between feminism and the person-centred approach.* Ross-on-Wye: PCCS Books.

Proctor, G, Cooper, M, Sanders, P & Malcolm, B (2006) *Politicizing the Person-Centred Approach: An agenda for social change.* Ross-on-Wye: PCCS Books.

Prouty, G, Van Werde, D & Pörtner, M (2002) *Pre-Therapy: Reaching contact-impaired clients.* Ross-on-Wye: PCCS Books.

Purton, C (1996) The deep structure of the core conditions: A Buddhist perspective. In R Hutterer, G Pawlowsky, PF Schmid and R Stipsits (eds)

Client-Centered and Experiential Psychotherapy: A paradigm in motion. Frankfurt am Main: Peter Lang, pp. 455–67.

Purton, C (2004a) Focusing-oriented therapy. In P Sanders (ed) *The Tribes of the Person-Centred Nation: An introduction to the schools of therapy associated with the person-centred approach.* Ross-on-Wye: PCCS Books, pp. 45–66.

Purton, C (2004b) *Person-Centred Therapy: The focusing-oriented approach.* Basingstoke: Palgrave.

Raskin, N (1948/2004) The development of nondirective therapy. *Journal of Consulting Psychology, 12,* 92–110. Reprinted in NJ Raskin (2004) *Contributions to Client-Centered Therapy and the Person-Centered Approach.* Ross-on-Wye: PCCS Books, pp. 1–27.

Raskin, N (2004) *Contributions to Client-Centered Therapy and the Person-Centered Approach.* Ross-on-Wye: PCCS Books.

Raskin, N (2005) The nondirective attitude. In BE Levitt (ed) (2005) *Embracing Non-directivity.* Ross-on-Wye: PCCS Books, pp. 329–47.

Rice, LN (1974/2001) The evocative function of the therapist. In DA Wexler & LN Rice (eds) *Innovations in Client-Centered Therapy.* New York: Wiley, pp. 289–311. Reprinted S Haugh & T Merry (eds) (2001) *Rogers' Therapeutic Conditions, Volume 2: Empathy.* Ross-on-Wye: PCCS Books, pp. 112–30.

Rogers, CR (1942) *Counseling and Psychotherapy.* Boston: Houghton Mifflin.

Rogers, CR (1951) *Client-Centered Therapy.* Boston: Houghton Mifflin.

Rogers, CR (1957) The necessary and sufficient conditions of therapeutic personality change. *Journal of Consulting Psychology, 21,* 95–103. Reprinted in H Kirschenbaum and VL Henderson (eds) (1990) *The Carl Rogers Reader.* London: Constable, pp. 219–35.

Rogers, CR (1959) A theory of therapy, personality and interpersonal relationships, as developed in the client-centered framework. In S Koch (ed) *Psychology: A study of science, Vol. 3: Formulations of the person and the social context.* New York: McGraw-Hill, pp. 184–256.

Rogers, CR (1961) *On Becoming a Person.* Boston: Houghton Mifflin.

Rogers, CR (1978) *Carl Rogers on Personal Power.* London: Constable.

Rogers, CR (1980) *A Way of Being.* Boston: Houghton Mifflin.

Rogers, CR (1986/2002) Reflection of feelings. *Person-Centered Review, 1* (4), 375–7. Reprinted in D Cain (ed) (2002) *Classics in the Person-Centered Approach.* Ross-on-Wye: PCCS Books, pp. 13–14.

Rogers, CR, Gendlin, ET, Kiesler, DJ & Truax, CB (1967) *The Therapeutic Relationship and its Impact: A study of psychotherapy with schizophrenics.* Madison: University of Wisconsin Press.

Sanders, P (ed) (2004) *The Tribes of the Person-Centred Nation: An introduction to the schools of therapy associated with the person-centred approach.* Ross-on-Wye: PCCS Books.

Sanders, P (2005) Principled and strategic opposition to the medicalisation of distress and all of its apparatus. In S Joseph & R Worsley (eds) *Person-Centred Psychopathology: A positive psychology of mental health.* Ross-on-Wye: PCCS Books, pp. 21–42.

Schmid, PF (1998) 'Face to face'. The art of encounter. In B Thorne & E Lambers *Person-Centred Therapy: A European perspective.* London: Sage, pp. 74–90.

Schmid, PF (2001) Comprehension: The art of not knowing. Dialogical and ethical perspectives on empathy as dialogue in personal and person-centred relationships. In S Haugh and T Merry (eds) *Rogers' Therapeutic Conditions, Volume 2: Empathy.* Ross-on-Wye: PCCS Books, pp. 53–71.

Schmid, PF (2004) Back to the client: A phenomenological approach to the process of understanding and diagnosis. *Person-Centered & Experiential Psychotherapies, 3* (1), 36–51.

Schmid, PF (2005) Authenticity and alienation: Towards an understanding of the person beyond the categories of order and disorder. In S Joseph & R Worsley (eds) *Person-Centred Psychopathology: A positive psychology of mental health.* Ross-on-Wye: PCCS Books, pp. 75–90.

Shlien, JM (1961/2003) A client-centered approach to schizophrenia: A first approximation. In A Burton (ed) *Psychotherapy of the Psychoses.* New York: Basic Books, pp. 285–317. Reprinted in JM Shlien (2003) *To Lead an Honorable Life.* Ross-on-Wye: PCCS Books, pp. 30–59.

Shlien, JM (1984/2003) A countertheory of transference. In JM Shlien & RF Levant (eds) *Client-Centered Therapy and the Person-Centered Approach.* Westport, CT: Praeger, pp. 153–81. Reprinted in JM Shlien (2003) *To Lead an Honorable Life.* Ross-on-Wye: PCCS Books, pp. 93–119.

Shlien, JM (1997/2001/2003) Empathy in psychotherapy: Vital mechanism? Yes. Therapist's conceit? All too often. By itself enough? No. In AC Bohart & LS Greenberg (eds) *Empathy Reconsidered.* Washington, DC: APA, pp. 63–80. Reprinted in S Haugh and T Merry (eds) (2001) *Rogers' Therapeutic Conditions, Volume 2: Empathy.* Ross-on-Wye: PCCS Books, pp. 38–52. Reprinted in JM Shlien (2003) *To Lead an Honorable Life.* Ross-on-Wye: PCCS Books, pp. 173–90.

Sommerbeck, L (2003) *The Client-Centred Therapist in Psychiatric Contexts: A therapists' guide to the psychiatric landscape and its inhabitants.* Ross-on-Wye: PCCS Books.

Sommerbeck, L (2005) An evaluation of research, concepts and experiences pertaining to the universality of CCT and its application in psychiatric settings. In S Joseph & R Worsley (eds) *Person-Centred Psychopathology.* Ross-on-Wye: PCCS Books, pp. 317–36.

Spandler, H (1996) *Who's Hurting Who?* Manchester: 42nd Street.

Stiles, WB, Barkham, M, Twigg, E, Mellor-Clark, J & Cooper, M (2006) Effectiveness of cognitive-behavioural, person-centred and psycho-dynamic therapies as practised in UK National Health Service settings. *Psychological Medicine, 36,* 555–66.

Thorne, B (1992) Psychotherapy and counselling: The quest for differences. *Counselling, 3* (4), 242–8.

Thorne, B (1985/1991) *The Quality of Tenderness.* Norwich: Norwich Centre Publications. Reprinted in B Thorne (1991) *Person-Centred Counselling: Therapeutic and spiritual dimensions.* London: Whurr, pp. 73–81.

Thorne, B (1998) *Person-Centred Counselling and Christian Spirituality: The secular and the holy.* London: Whurr.

Thorne, B (1999) Psychotherapy and counselling are indistinguishable. In C Feltham (ed) *Controversies in Counselling and Psychotherapy.* London: Sage, pp. 225–32.

Thorne, B & Lambers, E (eds) (1998) *Person-Centred Therapy: A European perspective.* London: Sage.

Tudor, K (2000) The case of the lost conditions. *Counselling, 11* (1), 33–7.

Van der Veen, F (1970) Client perception of the therapist conditions as a factor in psychotherapy. In JT Hart and TM Tomlinson *New Directions in Client-Centered Therapy.* Boston: Houghton Mifflin, pp. 214–22.

Van Werde, D & Morton, I (1999) The relevance of Prouty's Pre-Therapy to dementia care. In I Morton (ed) *Person-Centred Approaches to Dementia Care.* Bicester: Winslow Press, pp. 139–66.

Warner, MS (1997) Does empathy cure? A theoretical consideration of empathy, processing and personal narrative. In AC Bohart & LS Greenberg (eds) *Empathy Reconsidered.* Washington, DC: APA, pp. 124–40.

Warner, MS (2002) Psychological contact, meaningful process and human nature. In G Wyatt and P Sanders (eds) *Rogers' Therapeutic Conditions, Vol. 4: Contact and Perception.* Ross-on-Wye: PCCS Books, pp. 76–95.

Warner, MS (2005) A person-centered view of human nature, wellness and psychopathology. In S Joseph & R Worsley *Person-Centred Psychopathology: A positive psychology of mental health.* Ross-on-Wye: PCCS Books, pp. 91–109.

Whelton, W & Greenberg, LS (2002) Psychological contact as dialectical construction. In G Wyatt and P Sanders (eds) *Rogers' Therapeutic Conditions, Volume 4: Contact and Perception.* Ross-on-Wye: PCCS Books, pp. 96–114.

Wilkins, P (2003) *Person-Centred Therapy in Focus.* London: Sage.

Wilkins, P (in press) *Researching Person-Centred Therapy.* Ross-on-Wye: PCCS Books.

Worsley, R (2004) Integrating with integrity. In P Sanders (ed) *The Tribes of the Person-Centred Nation: An introduction to the schools of therapy associated with the person-centred approach.* Ross-on-Wye: PCCS Books, pp. 125–48.

Wyatt, G (2000/2001) The multi-faceted nature of congruence within the therapeutic relationship. *Person-Centered Journal, 7* (1), 52–68. Reprinted in G Wyatt (ed) (2001) *Rogers' Therapeutic Conditions, Volume 1: Congruence.* Ross-on-Wye: PCCS Books, pp. 79–95.

Wyatt, G (2001) (ed) *Rogers' Therapeutic Conditions, Volume 1: Congruence.* Ross-on-Wye: PCCS Books.

Wyatt, G & Sanders, P (eds) (2002) *Rogers' Therapeutic Conditions, Volume 4: Contact and Perception.* Ross-on-Wye: PCCS Books.

Zimring, F (2000/2001) Empathic understanding grows the person … *Person-Centered Journal, 7* (2), 101–13. Reprinted in S Haugh and T Merry (eds) (2001) *Rogers' Therapeutic Conditions, Volume 2: Empathy.* Ross-on-Wye: PCCS Books, pp. 86–98.

INDEX

actualising tendency 17, 25–32, 68, 85
Allport, GW 16, 115
anxiety 21, 29, 85, 90, 97, 105–7
Axline, V 101, 115
Aykroyd, M 38, 116

Baker, N 15, 115
Barley, DE 105, 117
Barrett-Lennard, GT 15, 28, 56, 57, 67, 69, 76, 77, 98, 103, 115
Baughan, R 73, 115
BEHAVIOURISM/ist 26, 67–8, 104
Bentall, R 113, 114, 115, 116, 118
BLRI 67, 76, 77
bodily changes 90
Bohart, AC 64, 72, 79, 91, 92, 93, 106, 115
Bond, T 112, 116
Bowlby, J 34, 115
Boy, AV 47, 115
Boyles, J 101, 115
Bozarth, JD 60, 71, 110, 115
Breggin, P 101, 116
British Association for the Person-Centred Approach (BAPCA) 100, 101, 109
Brodley, BT 70, 71, 81, 82, 83, 116
Bryant-Jefferies, R 100, 116
Burdett, J 4, 116

Cameron, R 36, 37, 73, 116
child development 17–18
client
  as active self-healer 79, 91
  incongruence 43
  perception 41, 74, 76
Clinical Outcomes in Routine Evaluation-Outcome Measure (CORE) 105
Coffeng, T 40, 116

COGNITIVE BEHAVIOUR THERAPY (CBT) 91, 105, 106, 107
Combs, AW 22, 116
communication 35–6, 39–41, 65–6, 74–8
community 29
CONDITIONS OF WORTH 12, 18, 31–2, 59, 111
CONFIGURATIONS OF SELF 47, 62, 111
congruence 19, 43, 52, 56
contact (psychological)
  functions 38
  milieu 39, 40
  reflections 39, 40, 41
Cooper, M 15, 73, 102, 116, 118
Culley, S 112, 116

Davies, E 4, 116
Davies, N 38, 116
DEATH INSTINCT 27, 111
defence 20, 52
dementia 38, 40
DENIAL 20–1, 111
depression 2, 21, 46, 87–8, 105–8
DIALOGICAL approach 15, 72–3, 111
dissociative states 40
DISTORTION 20–1, 111
DRIVE theories 25–6, 28, 111, 112
Dryden, W 100

Ellingham, I 83, 116
Elliott, R, 104, 105, 107, 116
Embleton Tudor, L 28, 36, 110, 116
empathy 12, 22, 45, 65–73, 107–8
  evocative 70
  idiosyncratic 71
  reverberative 72
Evans, R 81, 116
expert/ise (counsellor as,) 8, 11, 22, 45, 52–4, 67, 80, 84–5

Facilitator Development Institute (FDI) 99

FOCUSING-ORIENTED (counselling) 15
formative tendency 32
Frankel, M 54, 116
Freeth, R 101, 116

Gaylin, N 35, 101, 117
Gendlin, ET 15, 69, 86, 119
Grant, B 68, 69, 82, 84, 117
Greenberg, LS 35, 72, 104,
    115, 116, 121

Harlow, HF 34, 117
Haugh, S 57, 110, 117
Henderson, VL 7, 23, 33, 38,
    42, 66, 102, 117
Hendrix, V 118
hierarchy of needs 27
holism 24
HOMOEOSTASIS 25, 26, 28, 112
humanism/istic 23
    PSYCHOLOGY 16, 26, 104, 112

incongruence 19, 43–50, 55, 59–60
individualism 29, 30, 112
instrumental
    application of conditions 11, 68
    non-directivity (see 'non-
        directivity')
integrative counselling 10, 11, 14–
    15, 84, 112
INTERNAL
    dialogue 44, 89
    FRAME OF REFERENCE 65, 112
INTROJECTED VALUES 18, 31, 59–60,
    97, 112, 113
INTROJECTION 59–60, 85, 112

Joseph, S 44, 47, 49, 110, 117

Keemar, K 28, 36, 110, 116
Kelly, GA 113, 117
Keys, S 101, 117
King, M 100, 105, 117
Kirschenbaum, H 6, 23, 33, 38, 42,
    66, 98, 102, 103, 109, 117

Lambers, E 49, 99, 117, 121
Lambert, MJ 105, 117
Lee, RR 114, 117
Lietaer, G 57, 104, 116, 117
LOCUS
    OF CONTROL 45, 85, 112
    OF EVALUATION 60, 112
love 27, 29, 32, 59–61, 75

Mahrer, A 112, 117
Maslow, A 26, 27, 118
Masson, J 63, 118
McLeod, J 113, 118
Mearns, D 15, 30, 44, 47, 61, 62,
    110, 118
MEDICAL MODEL 44–50, 87, 112, 113
Merry, T 14, 29, 61, 68, 73, 110, 118
Miller, MJ 101, 118
Mitchell, DL 36, 118
Moodley, R 73, 118
Morton, I 40, 121
Mosher, L 101, 118
Murphy, LJ 36, 118

Napier, MB 73, 118
National Association of Young
    People's Counselling
    (NAYPCAS) 99
National Institute for Health and
    Clinical Excellence (NICE)
    104, 106, 107
National Marriage Guidance
    Council 98
non-directivity 10–12, 14, 45, 68,
    78, 80–5
    instrumental 11, 12, 68, 82–3
    principled 11, 12, 14, 82–4
Norcross, JC 107, 118

O'Leary, C 101, 118
ORGANISMIC VALUING PROCESS 17–18,
    59–60, 113

palliative care 40
PERSONAL CONSTRUCTS 89, 90, 113

personality
  development 18, 32, 34–5, 70
  theory of 16–24
PHENOMENOLOGY 21–2, 45–6, 50,
  67, 113
Pörtner, M 38, 40, 118
pre-therapy 14, 38–9
presence 38, 42
PRIMARY PREVENTION RESEARCH 4, 113
principled
  provision of conditions 11, 14,
    68, 73, 83
  non-directivity (see 'non-
    directivity')
process 24, 86
  conception of psychotherapy/
    change 86–92
Proctor, G 73, 118
Prouty, G 38, 40, 118
PSYCHOANALYSIS 26–7, 67–8, 113
PSYCHODYNAMIC THERAPY 105, 113
psychological
  contact 7, 33–42, 78
  maturity 54
  tension 19, 20, 32, 113
PSYCHOPATHOLOGY 4, 44–50, 113
psychosis 34, 38, 40, 101, 113
Purton, C 15, 101, 118, 119

RANDOMISED CONTROLLED TRIAL
  (RCT) 104, 105, 113
Raskin, N 80, 81, 103, 118
Read, J 119
REDUCTIONISM 24, 104, 114
research 4, 10, 13, 15, 76–7, 91,
  98, 102–8
Rice, LN 71, 119
Rogers, CR 6, 16, 22, 23, 24, 28,
  29, 30, 31, 32, 33, 35, 38, 42,
  43, 51, 52, 53, 58, 59, 60, 61,
  62, 65, 66, 74, 76, 78, 80, 81,
  82, 85, 86, 87, 88, 90, 102,
  108, 119

Sanders, P 47, 70, 74, 98, 110, 119,
  121

SCHIZOPHRENIA 39, 46, 72, 75, 87,
  107, 113, 114
Schmid, PF 15, 69, 72, 84, 119, 120
SELF
  -actualisation 19, 26, 29–31, 55
  -CONCEPT 18–21, 90, 111, 112
  -PSYCHOLOGY 31
  -regard (positive) 59
  -STRUCTURE 19, 31, 59–60, 78
seven stages of process 87–8
SHADOW SIDE 23, 27, 114
Shlien, JM 35, 70, 72, 75, 120
Snygg, D 22, 116
SOCIALISATION 27–9, 31, 114
Sommerbeck, L 48, 54, 116, 120
Spandler, H 101, 120
Stiles, WB 105, 120

Tallman, K 79, 91, 106, 115
Thorne, B 30, 37, 47, 62, 99, 100,
  101, 110, 118, 120, 121
threat 20–1, 60, 78, 84
Tolan, J 110
Truax, CB 86, 119
Tudor, K 74, 110, 121

University of Chicago Counseling
  Center 98, 103
unconditional positive regard,
  (UPR) 8, 12, 41, 42, 58–64,
  74, 84

Van der Veen, F 77, 78, 121
Van Werde, D 38, 40, 118, 121

Walshaw, T 101, 117
Warner, MS 34, 35, 47, 49, 69, 70, 121
wax disc recordings 98
Whelton, W 35, 121
Wilkins, P 47, 49, 57, 63, 110, 121
WISCONSIN PROJECT 77, 86, 114
Worsley, R 15, 44, 47, 49, 110,
  117, 121
Wyatt, G 54, 74, 110, 121

Zimring, F 69, 121